Other books by Misha Ha Baka

Poetry
CONFESSIONS OF A LONELY MYSTIC small talk

CONFESSIONS
OF A
LONELY MYSTIC

SHORT TALK

CONFESSIONS
OF A
LONELY MYSTIC

SHORT TALK

Stories

By

MISHA HA BAKA

Confessions of a Lonely Mystic short talk

Published by Ha Baka Book

First edition paperback 2017

Dedication

For Mom
And in memory of
My Nephew,
Pop,
Grandparents,
And
Tiger.

Premonitions of a Time to Come

Where you think you are
Is not necessarily
Where you may be.
What you are seeing
May not be what others see.
What you ask for,
May come to you
In ways, you didn't foresee.
Dreams come true
To sometimes end.
What seems quite empty
Can have seams quite full.
Catch it quick,
It may soon be gone.
The obvious is not always
Quickly caught.
When all is lost,
Something may be found.
Sometimes what jingles
Is a familiar sound.
Not all that you see,
Is seen by all,
That see you.
Oh, lint I may,
Oh, lint I might,
Have you vanished
From my sight.
Polly doesn't always
Want a cracker,
Sometimes she likes
Finger food.
Who says a dream
Is just a dream?
Perhaps it is,
Just another chance?
Was that *who* or *whom*,
You said was calling?

STORIES

short talk

After publishing my first book, Confessions of a Lonely Mystic *small talk*, I sat staring at the screen of my laptop. I asked myself, "OK. What's next?" Immediately that inner voice within said, "Why not publish some of the short stories?" Not liking to argue with me because if either side wins, I also loose. (I know, just one of life's mysteries.) I pulled a few of them; ten to be exact and began compiling them into this collection. They reveal parts of my inner me; hence, they are still *confessions*. Sixteen years after *small talk,* I am still alone, hence *lonely*. And although I have now found God, I still consider myself a *mystic*. "You still have to chop water and carry wood," or however that Zen Ben Kohan goes. (You'll understand in the future.)

This collection reflects some of the unusual experiences that oftentimes cross my path with a minimum of literary devices. They are small samplings of short introductions to the mysteries of the universe made obvious in a natural way. I subtitled them *short talk* because they are short stories.

I hope you enjoy delving into parts of my inner me for a second time and I thank you for even being willing to do so again.

Misha Ha Baka

Café Musica

chapter one

Where you think you are
Is not necessarily where you may be.
And what you are seeing
May not be what others see.

I hate traveling alone.

Being single and uninvolved most of the time makes it difficult to travel with a partner. The I Ching or Chinese Book of Changes says, "When three travel, one is sure to go and when one travels alone, he is sure to find a companion." It appears companions come in various forms. Little did I know what form mine was to take, but for certain, I was to find out.

Mexico is a delightful country. I had been there once before when I was a teenager. It was the summer of 1969. My best buddy Robert and I decided to hitch to Mexico. The USA was a different country then. People were still innocent and strangers were still safe.

We made our way out of New York City, which was a necessity since even then, it was an entity on to itself. It was different than the rest of the country. Once out of NYC, we were immediately able to hitch our way across the country. Most of the trip seems like a blur to me except for a few salient experiences which still remain present in my mind. The first of which was a night with the ponies.

Night of the Ponies

When hitching at the roadside, one never knows who will stop to pick you up. We were incredibly fortunate during the entire trip. I remember the tall man from Texas who wore a cowboy hat, boots, owned a van and a Shetland pony farm. He drove us to his farm. Dozens of miniature horses made their perfumed presence pungently noticeable. He let us spend the night in the very same mini-van that he had picked us up in.

The night was a sleepless one. We spent it in sleeping bags, which were pulled tightly over our heads, so the hordes of flies would be kept away from our faces. With the temperature reaching high up into the eighties, they served as a personal sauna.

The experience was similar to the night I spent on a beach in Eilat. The local youth hostel was filled to capacity, so I needed to find other accommodations. I was young and fearless. I walked down to the beach. I unpacked my parka and pulled it tight over my head to keep the flies away. It seems over the years flying things seem to occasionally plague me, but that's another story. Back to the *horseys,* as my nephew used to say before he passed on.

We rose early since we couldn't sleep. The next thing I remember about the trip is that harrowing drive to the border town. Two inebriated individuals with a beer cooler in the back picked us up and put us through the most treacherous ride of my life. Fortunately, we arrived safely. Most probably thanks to the Grace of God because it definitely wasn't due to their driving skills.

Don't ask me which border town. It's been a while, but I do remember I kept telling Robert, "Be sure you don't drink the water. It's unsafe, don't drink the water!"

We had been traveling for quite a while. We were hungry and craved a decent meal. Our student budget necessitated that we pick a fast-food stop for dinner. It was there that we learned about one of the national treasures of the country. As we approached the entrance to a café, the largest cockroach we had ever seen started crossing our paths. Robert, being the brave one, immediately lunged forward to trash it with his foot. As he was about to squash the sucker, two huge men grabbed him by the armpits and raised him up high with feet still dangling. Robert was a tall guy, 6'2" so you can only imagine the height on the two men that lifted him. They placed him down next to me. In a parental manner, they politely shook their indexes at us and said, "La Cucaracha, La Cucaracha. No, No, No!" We understood and walked into the restaurant with our hearts still racing.

We sat down and with extreme caution ordered carefully, being sure to omit the customary glass of water: Only cola and burgers for us, however, we were amiss. The colas came with ice. *Who would have thought that frozen water was also suspect?* This was a lesson not to be forgotten. It was one that saved me, from great discomfort, at an upscale restaurant during my second trip to that country. See, who said, "History repeats itself"?

Since we had eaten, it was now time for some entertainment. After all, we were on vacation and the trip of our lives. Music was what we craved. Not being capable of speaking in foreign tongues yet, in my best Spanish, I asked a stranger to direct us to a Café Musica. At least to me, that was what a music establishment might be called. And as they say, "Boy was I in for a surprise." In the future, history did repeat itself in a big way.

After many attempts and many inquiries, we finally succeeded in finding find someone who understood us, agreed to direct us and even escort us to our "Café Musica." He led us to what looked like a shady part of town. *What did we know?* We had just "gotten off of the boat," or more appropriately, vacated the pony farm.

We walked in. It was dark and the room was all red: Red curtains, red lights, smoke-filled and – music playing. *Wow*, we thought. *Not only music, but they were also dancing. So, so close?* We looked at each other slapping our hands in high-fives! We had hit pay dirt. It was then that the ladies started approaching us and tried to pull us off to the rooms located on the sides of the dance floor. It was also then we realized what this Café Musica really was. It was not just a musical café. Very gingerly, we tippy-toed out as quickly as we could, making sure that we didn't step on any *cucarachas*: Robert's armpits were still sore.

I don't remember sleeping much in México; however, thirty years do take their toll. Perhaps, had I remembered to take my Binka Galova, (I don't remember the correct spelling either.) I could have remembered more of the trip. I do have a faint recollection of spending a night at a second cousin's house. Of course, there was also that one night when I awoke with a companion on top of me.

Night of the Stinger

Since we didn't have a place to stay for that night, Robert surveyed the roadside for a place where we could lay out our sleeping bags. He located what seemed to be a safe place. We walked several yards off the road to a clear spot. We weren't at all concerned about the oncoming traffic since it was positioned directly behind three concrete roadside bunker barriers. The next thing I remember is waking up in the morning and seeing my new companion on top of me. No, this isn't an x-rated moment.

It was positioned directly dead center on my chest and was staring directly into my eyes. I deliberately breathed quite slowly. Panic began spreading throughout my body. I felt adrenaline shoot into my stomach. *What to do?* Fear elevated my pulse. Finally, I held that shallow breath I was breathing. Muscling up every last ounce of aim I could focus, I swiftly struck it with the backside of my right hand, slapping it off my chest. I had been sleeping with a scorpion. Not a Scorpio, a *scorpion*. Needless to say, I should have learned my lesson from the *Night of the Eyes*, but being in my teens, who paid any attention to details? Teens are invulnerable. Teens are impervious to minor annoyances such as wild animals or poisonous crawling creatures. "Right?"

Night of the Eyes

That night, two guys who thought it very funny to ditch us in the middle of nowhere, dropped us off on an empty road. Yes, even with innocence pervading the country, there was still maliciousness amidst the many. Luckily, we experienced much more beneficence then the converse. It was 2:00 a.m. Not even one car was traveling down that road. It was then that we saw them: A pair of eyes across the three-lane highway.

Spotlights couldn't have appeared any more blinding. At first, they were stationary. Then they slowly began to swerve back and forth, moving ever closer and then retreating back. They reminded me of the time I was driving in an unlit tunnel at night. A pair of headlights was on the other side of the road approaching me. I thought nothing of it until they then moved into my lane and started coming straight for me. Before I had a chance to freak out, they split apart. Two motorcyclists were having some fun at my expense: I had just gotten my license three weeks prior.

We couldn't figure out what we were looking at, or rather what was looking at us. Then the eyes began multiplying: At first two, then four, then eight and then twelve. An epidemic! That familiar panic began setting in. We quickly figured it out. At best, they were dogs, at worst wolves.

It could have been a fifty-fifty shot. After all, it could have gone either way. Why wolves? Perhaps they were only a pack of stray dogs. Wrong! From across the highway, the original pair started to move out of the darkness towards us until we could actually see their entire bodies. *Thank God* we thought, *it was a huge four lanes on each side highway.* We could tell first, *it* was scouting us, edging ever closer to the divider, and then moving back towards the pack. When two of them were almost at the curb, we were prepared to run. There were no cars in sight. They had now reached the highway. Calmly they started walking towards us. Of course, each step that they took in unison, for us, seemed to take an hour to pass. It was as if they knew that at this time of the night, only God traveled the highway. Tonight, at this particular moment, it looked like God was very busy taking a different route.

Things can change in an instant and sometimes God appears in the guise of a woman. Yes, they must have instituted equality upstairs a long time before a woman ran for president down here. It was at that very moment that a woman, who had a daughter, who just happened to also be hitching, stopped right between the wolves and us.

She rolled the passenger side window down and asked, "Do the two of you need a ride?"

I looked at Robert. Robert looked at me. We both peered through and around the car to see if the wolves were approaching. They had vacated the premises. In unison, we said: "Yes, thank you so much!" Our hearts returned to our chests.

"As we speak, my daughter is doing the very same thing that you are doing. She is hitching through California with her girlfriend."

Once in the car, since there wasn't enough room for all of *them* anyway, we could clearly see the entire pack had retreated quickly. It did take a lot longer for our hearts to settle back down since for a while they had been hanging out in our throats. I don't remember exactly where she took us, but she dropped us off somewhere in Houston.

You heard what?

My second trip to Mexico was spent traveling alone. The financial constrictions that I had while I was a student were long gone. I now had achieved a greater degree of financial well being, which this time, allowed me to afford to sleep at a plush hotel. I gave up my scorpion laden sleeping bag for a comfortable bed. Not even for a fleeting moment did I miss the humble roadside accommodations of my teenage years. This trip was uneventful, well almost. I did the tourist thing. I took day trips to various locations and searched for empowered places. I met a lovely couple from Ireland that persisted in keeping in contact with me for years after the trip.

I hadn't met anyone on the trip that I could really relate to, especially, of course, women. That is if you don't count the one I saw in the lobby.

I had forgotten to specifically request a room away from the elevators. Flies and elevator bells seemed to plague me at times. If I didn't specifically request a room away from the floor elevator, the concierge would put me right on top of it, right next to it or even, right in front of it. They like getting rid of the worst rooms first. It was as if the person that seated you at the restaurant wanted to put you at the worst possible table even when the restaurant was empty. I suspect they have their instructions and the instructors all attended the same class: Single people *do not count*, so dump them wherever. I made sure I didn't accommodate them by stating my preferences on the onset when I could remember of course. But since I kept forgetting to take my Binko Galova, I remembered when I was already in my room. Since it was just for one night, I figured, *hey, what the heck!*

I was being picked up by a tour bus in the morning, figured *I could* rough it *being next to the elevator*. In reality, I was too lazy to go back down to the lobby and get another room. The things we think to justify the things we want and do not want to do. *Spoiler alert*: "Famous last words." It had been an exhausting trip. Of course, as soon as I had lain down and closed my eyes, then "it" started. If "it" had been during the holidays, then it might have been acceptable. "Who doesn't like hearing the occasional jingle and jangle of holiday bells?" But this was incessant. The doors opened and they jingled. The doors shut and they jangled. The doors opened and they jingled. The doors shut and they jangled. The doors opened and they jingled. The doors shut and they jangled. Over and over, you most probably get the gist of it by now.

Needless to say, I slept very little that night. Even when the elevators weren't jangling my nerves, I still had ringing in my ears. I couldn't wait to get out of the room. I hoped the next part of my journey would be more peaceful and pleasant. I packed and headed down to the lobby. I got out of the elevator one last time and waited to hear the jingle. Nothing. *Strange* I thought. I went over to the cashier and checked out. As I was about to leave, I couldn't resist complaining about the loudness of the elevator's bells. So I started talking to the cashier when she stopped me and pointed me in the direction of the Concierge's desk. She said, "Please discuss it with him."

I did as she asked. I went right over to the desk. He had his back turned to me when I approached. Then he deliberately slowly turned towards me. His waxed, sculptured mustache screamed, "I am a professional and am very proud of what I do!" He looked at me and with one of those winning, charming, totally fake smiles and said, "Senior, what can I do for you?"

I said, "Sir, I just want you to know the room was excellent. Last night, the meal was superb. But I do have just one small complaint."

"Sir, please do tell us. We want your experience in Mexico to be just perfect." He smiled while simultaneously throwing daggers at me with his eyes. Some people are so oblivious to the unmistakable fact that their facial expression can be easily read and deciphered. His screamed, "I am a liar; I am not even mildly interested in what you have to say to me. Not in the slightest. Why don't you go back to where you come from as quickly as you can. Perhaps even sooner, Gringo!"

I said, "I have been in many hotels, (which by the way was true,) but I have never heard anything more annoying than those elevator bells. They kept me up the entire night."

His whole demeanor and facial color changed. If this was a cartoon, his curled up mustache would have uncurled and shot out linearly to form a straight line. He scrunched his eye; left eye to be exact, tilted his head ever so slightly to the right, opened his mouth slightly with his upper lip also lifting to the left and said,

"Senior, this hotel's elevators do not have any bells. They do not have any buzzers; they make absolutely no sound whatsoever when the doors open, close or move from floor to floor. I am very sorry to have to tell you that you are very mistaken. Perhaps you were dreaming and thought it wasn't a dream?"

I couldn't move a muscle. I must have stopped breathing. I must have frozen long enough for him to touch me on my left shoulder and say, "Senior, are you OK?"

I came out of it and said, "Yes." I walked away without saying anything to him. I was at a loss. I had wanted to have *special* experiences during my trip, but I had never really expected to have any. Well, it looks like I just had my first. As they say, "Good things happen in threes."

Now you see me, now you don't!

The tour bus was picking me up shortly, but I had an hour or so to come to myself after hearing bells that silently sounded, but noisily jingled. I was still speechless. I sat down on a couch right in front of the souvenir shop. I thought *wouldn't it be nice to come home with a memorable souvenir from Mexico.* It was then I looked up. I saw perhaps one the most beautiful woman I had ever seen. She was parading across the lobby floor within a few feet of me. *If only I could catch a whiff of her perfume, I would be able to remember her forever.*

I watched her parade across and then my attention span must have drifted because as she approached a particular spot on the carpet she seemed to vanish. Then I would catch a glimpse of her again at the exact spot I had spotted her the first time. She would then proceed across the corridor of the hotel, only to somehow vanish again at its end. I thought *maybe she is walking into a store at the end and coming back out of it in the front?*

The mind tries explaining whatever it sees even if it really doesn't have an adequate explanation of what is actually occurring. I had no idea. I knew I was attracted to this beautiful woman and somehow she was there and then somehow she wasn't. Of course, all three were true, I was attracted to her, she was there and then she wasn't. Perhaps you can explain it to me? That hotel had many extras, which weren't advertised. That was number two and now for number three.

Café Musica Revisited

I decided to do the real "Café Musica" thing this time. I wanted to visit a restaurant, which had a mariachi band, on the day before I was to return home.

I was in Mexico City. After an hour or so of walking around in the tourist area, I found a place that looked like it might satisfy my musical and culinary requirements. I waited on line to get in and was seated towards the back. This time I didn't mind being placed there. The singer was exceptional, and the band played superbly. What a real treat! In unison, all of them roamed around from table to table singing and playing. I was truly impressed by their hi-tech approach. The singer carried a microphone with no cable. The band was loud enough and didn't need amplification.

I ordered one of my usual fare for Mexican cuisine: Those soft tortillas filled with salad and things. The food was excellent and the music, both heavenly and divine. I was content and was a very happy puppy. Finally, after thirty years I had experienced my *Café Musica*. I decided to tip the band. As I was leaving I took a five-peso coin out and walked right up to the singer, who at the moment wasn't singing. I reached for his hand and touched it. He turned to me startled. I looked him square in the eyes and in my best Spanish said, "Excellent job!" I gave him the thumbs up and then slipped the coin into his hand as I closed his fingers around it. He was still startled and just kept looking puzzled: At me and then at the coin, at me and then at the coin. *Perhaps he never received a tip before? Perhaps he thought the tip was too small? Who knows what goes through the mind of a gifted artist and performer.* I couldn't read minds in Spanish, yet. I loved his huge sombrero. I felt wonderful. I was having a really good day. It couldn't get much better. (Drum roll.)

On the way out, I walked over to the Maître D' and said, "Senior, thank you for the wonderful meal."

"Si, Senior."

"Thank you for the wonderful music."

"Si, Senior."

"And I especially thank you for that wonderful singer!"

He looked at me with the same puzzling look that the singer had greeted me with. I thought *maybe they were related?* It was then he said a few words that changed everything. Funny how four words can rock your world? Funny how four words can alter reality as you know it and transform the mundane into a slice of Heaven. I will always remember those four words.

He said, "But, Senior, we have no singer?"

OK, six words, but who is counting?

I suppose *they* are just as curious about us as we are of them. I suppose that given the ability to adorn themselves in any accouterment that they choose, then why not choose something bigger than life and appropriately colorful. I suppose the singer was just as shocked at realizing I could see him as I was at finding out that who I had been listening to was not being heard or seen by anyone else in the room or so I assumed. For sure, he wasn't on the playbill.

Mexico was a wonderful vacation spot. I loved the country, the food, the music, and the people. All of them! I have gone back there again, however, subsequently on occasion I did wonder, *how did he spend that five-peso coin?*

Markers

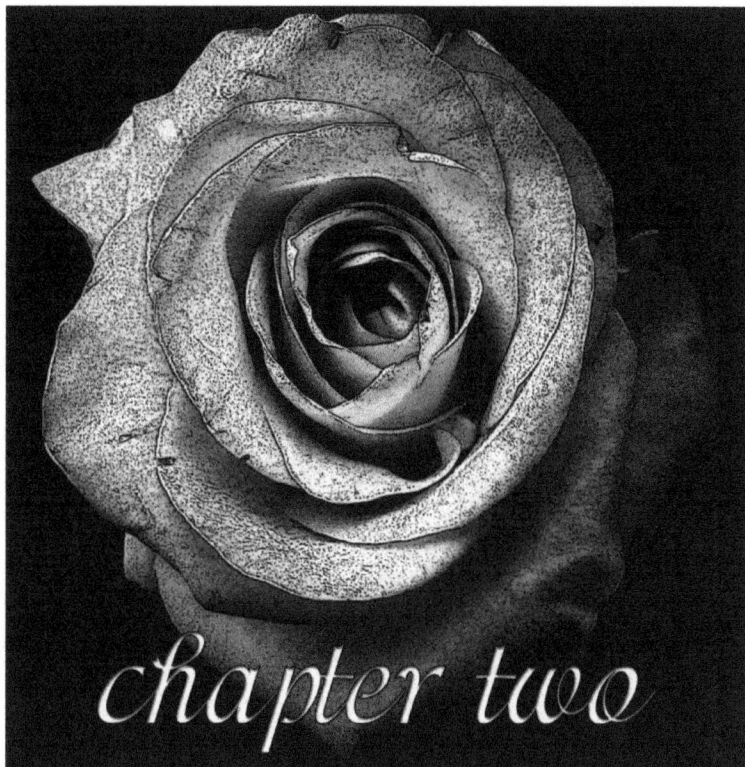

chapter two

What you ask for,
May come to you in ways
You didn't foresee.

Health, like illness, sometimes occurs due to unusual circumstances.

October 15 was the last night that I slept uninterruptedly this year. The night after that was the beginning of a nightmare that even lasts until I now write, which is five months later.

Family, holidays, sanctuary, protection, and love are all synonymous words with returning home for the holidays. In my case, these are the Jewish High Holy days. Counting all the trains I would have to take, my trip "home" was a multiple hour journey. I love trains. I leave the driving to them and the time to relax and work for me. The other passengers in a car can sometimes be a bit unnerving, but there are headphones for that.

I even have a standard position I assume when aboard a long train ride. It is almost a sitting fetal position: Legs go up with knees bent and pressed into the seat before me. Of course, they are carefully positioned in order not to jostle the passenger sitting in front of me. *Who needs disgruntled people sending bad vibes at you during the entire trip?* Some people live for such an opportunity. My body is slouched low and my back bent. Perhaps it is due to years of playing classical style guitar, or perhaps an inherited congenital weakness, but my back is rounded near the shoulders. Sitting so is quite a natural position for me.

My posture has always been poor. I felt awkward in my body. When it came time to pose for a picture, eleven times out of ten my head is always tilted to the left. Don't ask me why. Pop had to teach me how to walk. He showed me to let my arms swing. Up until then, I walked with them frozen. To no avail, Mom desperately tried to teach me how to stand up straight or sit up straight, she still does. They both tried getting me to walk around with a pole behind my back and hands bracing it. Of course, I pursued none of these wise suggestions because stubbornness runs in the family.

Once so positioned in the train car, I can maintain this posture for quite a while. At least until the legs fall completely asleep. Sometimes I enter a deep meditation and drift off for many moments. The train prepares me for my encounters with the folks and the family. It gives me an opportunity to soak up universal assistance so that I am better able to withstand the "nuances" of family interactions. I can also catch up with the latest techno-trends and recent spiritual revelations while riding. At times, the next part of the journey, having "arrived" is not quite as comfortable. But I am not alone with this. I've heard that's why alcohol was invented. Too bad I never drink.

Captive audience. That is the easiest way to describe it. At my age and having both parents still alive at the time of this writing is the exception rather than the rule. Given the difficulties both have lived through, perhaps it isn't a surprise. I call them my *exception magnets.* Since you ask, "Why do you call them that?" I, of course, won't hesitate to explain by giving two simple, but very clear examples of "Exceptionism." Don't be surprised if you have never heard of this word, I've been making words up since childhood. I coined "goo-goo-ga-ga" and wrote a book report on the *Religional* Beliefs of Greece in grade school, much to the chagrin of my 4th grade English teacher.

Mom

During my colored pencil painting series, I painted a portrait of Mom. I painted it photorealistically, down to each individual lash on her eyebrows, or at least I thought so. So now enter the parents in one of their *rare* visits to me in the city. Since of course, it is the duty of children to visit their parents *all* the time and not vice versa. The real reason for them not visiting often was Pop's total obsession with a fear of not being able to find a parking spot near my apartment. This was totally unwarranted since there was not even one occasion when they hadn't found a parking spot on my block and near my apartment immediately upon their arrival. I mentally reserved the spaces for them.

With the usual talks and entertaining tales, yes, I am the consummate storyteller, my role in the family; I displayed an exhibit of my latest work. With due fanfare, preparation and depredations, I produced the piéces de résistance, the new painting of Mom.

The drum rolls sound; both their glasses get cleaned. Like a fine-tuned engine or Swiss clock, the "exceptionism" motor begins to *rev* up. If you were there, then you would be able to hear centuries of refinement of the genetic and culturally passed down qualities of discernment of minutia. I suppose that when as a person or people, if you are found wanting, then whatever is found is wanted to be perfect.

Eyes squint and glasses are adjusted and readjusted, they also are never perfect. The conversation momentarily shifts away from the task at hand and turns to their ailments. Of course, too much attention has already been spent away from their comfort zone. Then after a polite prompt, the clearing of the throat trick didn't work. It only prompted an in-depth examination of my current physical health, which was something I didn't want to get into. Then finally after a while, a "walk up" occurs. A "walk around" occurs, like roosters hunting a hen, or wolves drooling over roaming sheep, a pronouncement is about to be vocalized.

I know that sinking, nervous feeling well: The one in the pit of your stomach. The one that wells up and encompasses you when every inch and iota of your being knows that something is going to occur soon, which in all likelihood will affect you in a negative way. Like arthritic prone people being able to sense a coming storm, or a waiter knowing they are going to get stiffed, I wait with breath held and stomach tensed so as to not get punched to badly in the gut. And then it comes. Then the moment of judgment arrives and is handed out like a foreman of a jury delivering their summary deliberation.

"It's nice…but why is that eyebrow crooked?"

The drum and symbol clap and bang, quite quickly and lasting for a moment before they drift out, stage left.

The event is over...the pronouncement has been made: *Less than perfect*. By the hair of a brow, nonetheless; one small step for improvement and one giant step for lack of satisfaction.

My father breathes a sigh of relief, "A mistake!"

She was right. The brow was uneven. It was not perfectly defined. There were gaps, which were visibly quite discernible. I had painted it photorealistically. So that was the way it really looked: Her eyebrows were not penciled in.

"You should have fixed it."

In hindsight, I could have, but that would have been like adding an untrue detail to this story. I could have written yes I fixed it after being asked to do so; however, it still hangs on her wall as is. I discussed it with her the other day. I told her about having written about the painting and her response to it upon having shown it to her. Immediately her finger went to the gap on the brow and said, "Yes, it is still crocked." I smiled.

Pop

Pop is similar, but in a different way: Much more creative in his treatment or dare I say mistreatment of an event of potential joy.

Fall is my favorite season. I love the temperature, the colors and the transition from summer. This was a difficult fall since I was unemployed, again. Needless to say, it was a period of great financial duress and stress. I try talking with God about my happiness and success, but it seems my periods of discomfort draw me ever-closer to him. I needed money and needed a clear indication that I was, in fact, walking on the right path. God also finds quick and easy ways to answer my requests; at least he has done so in the past.

That night, depressed and destitute I went for a walk along Broadway. Walking is good for me. It gives me time to meditate, ponder life's vicissitudes and do something, even if it isn't much. It was a fall night, not too cool, but it was breezy. I walked with my chin down, a common pose for me. Before I was "recently released," someone at the office had told me that I was a humble person. Obviously, that pose was one which I often assumed when I walked. Interestingly, I wasn't even aware of it until I was told. That night, I indeed did feel humble and humbled. I was at the bottom; even the pennies that I had been collecting were turned in for dollars and were now gone. In a cliché, I was penniless – literally.

Then I happened upon one of God's gifts. A wind, the kind that causes leaves to swirl in dance, or a bag to ballet its way across the street, sweeps a bill directly under my right foot. I lift my foot and see it is a twenty! Under the right foot of course, since I was on the right path. Mind you; I have lived in the city for decades. Money does not grow on trees any more than it appears under your foot it is a gift.

My downturned chin turned from down to up. I looked up at the dark starless night. You can't see stars in the city except for the occasional planet. Why we think God lives in the clouds is beyond me. I smiled and thanked God in my most fervent manner. I repeat the exact words here in the event the reader needs guidance on how to address God when a twenty appears under their right shoe while walking pennilessly on Broadway in the middle of a cool, fall night.

I said, "Thanks God."

Immediately I wanted to share the delight of my good fortune. I am one of those that like to share good fortune and keep the other kind under wraps. Also, being partnerless as usual; the only ones I have to call are the folks or my sibling. The folks got the nod. I called. After several moments of usual the usual chitchat I prepared to reveal the miracle that had just occurred. Of course, I did so with great anxiety and apprehension, as I would have hated having this great moment spoiled. There were so few in the past few months that could even mildly compare to this. But a man is not always from the Staten Island, I believe the saying goes that way, please don't quote me on that.

Pop gets on the phone; Mom is not far behind him. I reveal the night's events. And with anticipatory breath, I wait. The silence is deafening. One can hear the cogs and wheels of thousands of years of heritage churning. One can smell the scent of an "exceptionism" being brewed and about to be dished and poured out. And then it comes. The drum roll sounds again and the cymbal clangs, however this time it is a huge, huge Chinese gooooooooooong that reverberates and reverberates.

Pop speaks and says, "Be careful, don't spend it."

I pull my head back in wonder and confusion. My eyebrows are tensed and scrunched together. I twist my head to the right side and tilt it.

"Don't spend it? Why wouldn't I want to spend it?" I am baffled.

And then it comes. I never saw it coming. I doubt if anyone could have seen it coming. I doubt you can see it coming. "Can you?"

Pop speaks again and pronounces: "Don't spend it because it is counterfeit."

Mind you this is the only possible negative ramification to my newfound good fortune: A pronouncement that good fortune does not occur and if it looks like good fortune then it's not real. This was the spirituality that I was taught as a child; expect the worst and never trust the best. There are no miracles. How could there be? If there were miracles, would his immediate whole family have been murdered in the Holocaust? Would so many millions of Jewish people have been killed? I understood then and still do now: Love motivated the remark. It meant, "Don't set yourself up for disappointment. Don't hope for a better tomorrow. Hope is meaningless. Only trust in yourself and in what you can do for yourself. If six million weren't helped, how can you expect one in millions to receive help?"

Fortunately, I never succumbed to this line of thinking and feeling. Perhaps this is because my experience wasn't the same as those that had intimately felt the wrath of Nazi persecution. Despite my wavering moments, my belief and love of an invisible God still permeated my being and did not deter me from my quest to find him.

But, given all of this, it was my parents who helped me out of my financial woes. God bless parents that love you, even if they show it in abstruse ways. After all, if you don't know how to speak French, then you can only communicate in the language you were taught and grew up with. Life taught them how to survive during a war. How to overcome adversity, hunger, and cold. And how to overcome persecution and rise above the negativity of oppressive governments – to name but a few. No wonder the eyebrow was noticed as being crooked, it was. In that environment, the winds of ill fortune could twist a head, let alone an eyelash. The destitution of having to reach into barrels of garbage for some daily food. Only to be sick for days after having eaten worm-infested cheese. These experiences absolutely forbade finding anything of real value on city streets.

Pop did tell me something about God once. Something, which of course, later on, I was not going to listen to. But at the time, I had no idea, one day I would be in the position to do the exact opposite of what he was telling me not to do. Go figure how life puts things in your path even before the path is put in front of you.

Being a city boy, my parents do the driving when I arrive at their neck of the woods. It is not that I don't have a license, but more so, I don't own a car. They own an old large one; a luxury model. Pop drives and Mom directs, "Isn't that the way it is everywhere?" The ride to the restaurant or their home is a mini TV entertainment show. Perhaps, because of being the older sibling, I usually assume the burden of filling in the spaces and do most of the talking. This is regularly interrupted by Mom's persistent cough: An allergy, she claims. Allergy or not, after several moments in the car, I usually too feel a tickle or something in the throat. Over the years, with great perplexity, I have chalked it off to one thing or another. Pop, who also had issues. He was recuperating from some sort of virus, which rendered him sleepless, on and off. Neurologically it eventually even caused his loss of smell as well as hearing in one ear. Mom's complaint was constant irritation in her throat and dryness. In short, the car ride was an invitation to contagion. The things we do for love.

They live in a retirement complex in a duplex condo, which

was never stripped of its previous owner's incredibly bad sense of color. This prior owner may have been colorblind. Because otherwise there is absolutely no plausible explanation of how what was put together was put together in the manner that it was put together. Redundancy is the key here. I have my *own* room there. At least it used to be my own room until Pop adopted it as his second home. Mom needs her own bed, her own space. He needs his own place. Her coughing or her constant up and down trips to the facilities prompted him to retreat down to his own level, his "home within a home." His bed, of course, was filled with his emanations, sweat, health, and dis-health: A place that was soon to be my interim sleeping place.

Mom cooks: One part was her mom's recipes; one part was her innate creativity that often contributed to quite tasty a dish. A small part was my own cooking skills rubbing off upon her. There were some dishes she used to make that still make my mouth water when I think of them. Luckily for me, I was able to retrieve some of those recipes while she was able to remember them. There was also the unconscious cooking prep mannerism that added to the pot. Like how many times did you see a hostess with a severe cold taste the soup, several times with the same spoon to see if it is perfect? In short, Family shares many things, health and "not so health." My immune system must have also been off. So many years of smoking and city living didn't help either.

When I ate there, a sore usually formed in the lower right portion of my inner lip. I tried avoiding doing so, but the universe set it up to the contrary. How could one not eat at one's parent's house when you come to visit for the High Holy Days? It would be a sacrilege; it would be a "shondeh and a besheh" as is said in the vernacular and means a sacrilege and an embarrassment.

Thus enters the moral dilemma: I saw it coming. Which is it to be, their comfort or mine? A setup. From the perspective of the casual observer no potential harm; from my spiritual perspective, an opportunity to set me up for a fall. Of course, you ask, "Who is doing the setup?" Well as the Bard used to say, "There are more things..."

The night there was difficult. (Something I describe in greater depth in *The Night of the Marching Dead*.) My sleep was constantly interrupted by trips to the John, tossing and turning, lying awake, throat irritations, and labored breathing; I was soaking up their ill health, like a totally dehydrated and dry sponge sopping up liquid by the barrels. Mom would say, "You bring life into this house." She didn't realize it was literal; just another one of my blessings.

At work, I had been doing similarly so. I was surrounded by throat thingies: To the right of me someone with throat cancer, to the left someone with constant throat clearing; to her right chronic throat illness, and then others with constant coughing. My own throat was hoarse-like for a very long time.

Being oblivious to the physical with my head usually up in the clouds, or out of it focused on my art and music, I ignored the obvious. And so, for the first time in my life, predilection, opportunity, susceptibility, and setup aligned to produce a grand conjunction of disharmonious concatenations of susceptibility to the flu. Had I only spent one day and night there, I think I would have been OK, but guilt and stupidity prompted me to spend two. In America, the Jewish New Year was celebrated for two consecutive days: Twice the opportunity to be subjected to parental woes. I succumbed and stayed the second day. The second night clinched it; however, I didn't know that until two weeks later.

Being the glutton that I was, I actually returned the following week for a repeat performance on the Day of Atonement, the holiest day of the Jewish year. It was an additional opportunity to eat, sleep and contract. I actually volunteered for a second stint of availability for *dis-ease*. This time even coming home with a souvenir of a tick bite on my arm that I wouldn't notice for several days later. It was a done deal. Love and relationship had cost me money in the past. In one way or another, I had paid for moments of supposed emotional comfort or physical intimacy. Now I was to pay dearly again. Some situations repeat themselves. I did not make that saying up.

I love films, especially the animated ones. As a child, I would sit glued to the TV set watching those Saturday morning cartoons for hours. Since the advent of DVD (I was an early adopter.) I would purchase the ones I love or that looked interesting and I would stockpile them knowing they were instant cures for loneliness. The pile wouldn't last long since I often felt lonely. I'd marathon or binge watch them. It was rare for one to remain in the "to be viewed" pile for an extended period. Even more infrequent was the purchase of a foreign language subtitled film. I never seemed to be able to get into them. I did, however, purchase one, but to date, I haven't watched it. It is still sitting in my dual DVD player tray, with the cover next to me on a table.

It was while I was watching a movie on my home theater set-up that I experienced the first cough of the "flu-virus-thingy," which had been patiently waiting to introduce it's ugly head to me. I was lying on the floor when a long, deep whooping cough emerged. I had never felt or heard anything like it. Even the sound of it scared me. I actually looked around the room and asked, "What was that?" I half expected an answer from my guides: Spirit guides, for all of you that haven't yet talked to your unseen friends. It didn't reoccur so I resumed my film. I forget which one it was; I watch so many of them. I look at it as prep work for a future incarnation as a movie director/producer.

That night I awoke several times with a similar severe cough. My illness progressively worsened and I actually had to call out sick, something I have rarely done. My throat gradually became worse even to the point of laryngitis for several hours. My quest for medical assistance promptly began.

Over the years, I have rarely visited western MDs. If I actually did go, I would be truly very sick. A brief visit to the doc and penicillin was in my hands. I had taken it perhaps twice in my life.

This was my third time. I felt it clean out some sort of bacterial infection, but the throat-thingy was still there. Sleep was interrupted and sporadic. It was time to call in the troops; I was in search of an acupuncturist/herbalist. The Internet is a marvelous tool. Within minutes I had dozens to choose from. I found two and tried them for several weeks with no results. The throat thing was getting worse and the back of my neck and shoulders were throbbing too. I was beginning to get worried.

I tried every affirmation and healing meditation that I had learned as well as every technique for wellness being I could think of. Being desperate, I even made a statement to "call in markers from prior lives" to assist me. We may accrue brownie points in each lifetime. When we plan out our lives out prior to coming here, we include some of these to assist us. I was asking to cash in whatever chits were necessary, important, constructive and beneficial for me with ease, peace, and comfort that would heal and help me with what it was that I was then experiencing. I was calling in other's markers. I was calling for help from those who owed me because somewhere, in some way, I had helped them at sometime.

As I always do when I am worried, I turn to God. It was a day before Chanukah and a day before Christmas. They occurred concurrently this year and this year, I asked God for a specific present. I asked him to cure my situation and maintain my health. God responds to me.

On Christmas/Chanukah evening, during my evening meditation, and about fifteen minutes into it, I felt a presence. I have felt it before. It was a fullness, a heaviness, a tension, an uplifting, and an all-encompassing density. Then words formed...

On one of the High Holy Days, several years before, my father and I were sitting in the synagogue discussing God. "What else does one do when the Rabbi is off in *yeneh velt* (the other world) delivering a speech which makes absolutely no sense to anyone including himself." We had attended the same Orthodox Jewish synagogue since I was in the fourth grade.

I turned to my father and said, "Isn't it funny how so many people speak to God. And yet, when he speaks back to you, these very same people think you are crazy?"

He responded by saying, "No, you are only considered as being crazy if you tell someone he has spoken to you." Of course, neither of us were aware of the recent proliferation of books that were attributed to having been written by God and were currently flooding the bookstores.

That Christmas and Chanukah night the words I heard were from God; otherwise, someone else is calling me son. I won't repeat the words so that you won't have the opportunity to label me or to revere them, but the gist was quite simple: I deserved to be healed, and the healing would be maintained. It was then the fullness permeated my chest cavity and throat and in a scene not dissimilar to one in a popular film about a healer, I heaved the throat-thingy out of me several times. The last time I momentarily blacked out for several seconds, at least so it seemed. (This happened to me several times again later in life, with the first time resulting in me totaling my car and barely walking away unharmed by the skin of my teeth. Do not evacuate spirits while you drive!) The throat-thingy was gone. I was cured.

The next day at work, it returned. I was dumbfounded. I had been healed and it returned? Then that night during my meditation, again I felt the presence. I heard the words, "It will be maintained." It was followed by a vibrational (I know. I make up words, and have been doing so since childhood.) release in the throat area. This release occurred several times. Once again, it was gone.

Only to return again and again. I felt destitute, however, I had learned a technique to clear it up, albeit temporarily. I would wake at night and produce the *vibrational* evacuation, trying to disguise this sonic release with a full speed humidifier, AC or TV. Small paper-thin walls of an apartment necessitated that. This process continued and continued.

At this point, it had become a way of life with me. I learned how to function with it. I decide to have dinner at a health food restaurant, which I frequently had visited over the years. After arriving, and as I proceeded to visit the facilities, I ran into some old friends whom I hadn't seen for more than six years. They proceeded to tell me that due to illness, they were using a gifted

Peruvian healer who had previously proven successful for them. At this point, I was thought *I would try whatever would help me with ease, peace, and comfort.* Not that God didn't heal me, but for some reasons as of yet unbeknownst to me, it wasn't a done deal. We arranged to have dinner next week to discuss it further. I was very curious.

The following week, we met for dinner as planned. I learned the condition my friends were being treated for had now cleared up. A brief explanation of how the healer worked and what her energies were like, followed. Then something was said, that only clicked in with me several hours later. When it finally did, it made total sense to me why I hadn't previously been cured by God.

You see I had asked God to heal me after I had already called in the "markers." Energy, once released must manifest itself. Had I not called in the "markers," I would already have been cured at this point. Having called in "markers," I had to wait for the "markers" to manifest. My friends told me with viruses the healer did something very strange. Even for me, it would appear to be strange. I was dumbfounded as to what was about to come next.

I asked, "OK. What did she do?"

"She draws *markings* over the spot where the virus is."

My friends continued, "Even for us it was strange, but it worked.

I asked for her number. The next day I proceed to call her up, *I wondered if she was in.* She answered the phone; *she was in.* I had called in the Marker. I saw her that night.

Night of the Marching Dead

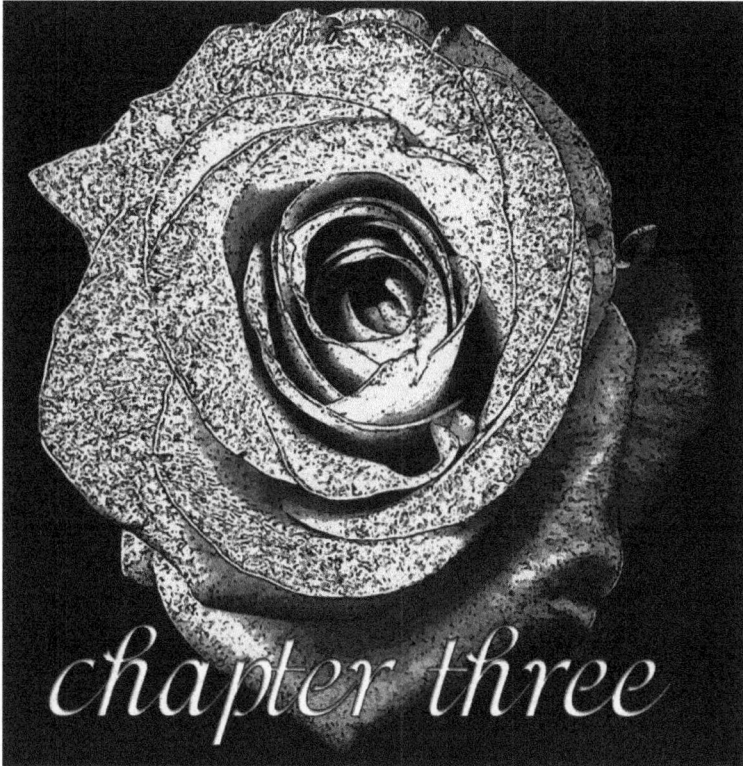

chapter three

Dreams come true,
And then they can end.
What seems quite empty
Can have seams quite full.

Chanukah is the festival of lights. It is a time of miracles and a holiday of giving and a holiday of receiving. It is filled with moments of joy, happiness and for some, even the unexpected. Light and darkness can sometimes have a fine line dividing them.

Living in a retirement village has its pluses and minuses. Residents are of similar stations in life, but people there who are no longer living can pose population control issues.

The ride up to *Happy Achers* (in pain, but still happy) is usually a comfortable one. My folks, my sibling and family all live in the same vicinity. It is easy to fall asleep on a moving train. The key is to stay awake until the conductor collects the tickets otherwise you have to wake and then it's a bit more difficult to lull oneself into a meditative sleep afterward. Following a long day at the office and especially since it was Friday, I had absolutely no difficulty entering *la-la land* after my ticket was collected. Since I am also a seasoned train-riding veteran, having made many such trips, I had become quite adept at sleeping with my music playing quite loud.

Before the train ride had begun, I had a sense to avoid a group of three men who were waiting to board my train. I casually glanced at them and they appeared to be three priests, with collars intact. I swore to myself they were three priests. I imagined *they must be heading to a retreat or their families for the holidays?* A survival trick at the rail station is to stand off to the side of the entrance to the track when the train arrives. Doing so avoids the crush of the incoming rush-hour crowd and temporarily avoids the onslaught of the departing passengers. Once the passengers de-trained, I pressed forward, wanting to grab a good seat. I anticipated a Friday evening's train ride during the holidays would produce a filled-to-capacity train. Of course, upon entering, as fate would have it, I choose the car where the three "priests" were seated. Mind you; I have nothing against priests. (I am an ordained member of the clergy.) I quickly pulled my belongings together and moved to another car, several cars up front. This I did because I found three people traveling together talked a lot. I like my silence when aboard the train. I also like a row with three seats. This way there was a greater likelihood that the middle seat would remain vacant.

So there I was, comfy in my seat and of course hoping the universe would provide an early Chanukah gift for me. Perhaps in the form of a beautiful, single, available, healthy woman to occupy the seat right next to me. Hasn't happened often I might add, but I've always been an optimist at heart. And yet, there was that one time in the airplane when I was returning home from Greenland.

Greenland

I had just completed a two-week stay there. It was wonderful: A three-day consulting gig, which paid for the entire two-week trip and then some. I was in heaven. Now, all that I needed was a sexy redhead to sit down next to me on the plane. I played that game often. I eagerly eyed the passengers who were going to board, searching for my beloved. Then, there she was, wearing a huge large hat. I almost thought that I was having a vision as I did in Café Musica. She looked larger than life, not that she was huge, she wasn't, she was perfect, but the look of her seemed divinely orchestrated. Such is the life of one such as me.

She was dressed in a tight-fitting black dress, high heels, and the whole nine yards. I told myself, *she was perfect*. Of course, I was dreaming with eyes-wide-open.

What were the odds she would sit next to me on the plane and I would start conversing with her? *Zilch, nada, nothing* I thought to myself. The flight attendants called for all of us to board the plane. At that point, knowing it was a fruitless reverie; I had already given up on keeping track of her. I boarded the plane and as I passed the one seat in front of where I was to sit – there she was, on my side of the plane, in my row, in the seat right next to me! I know you are as dumbfounded now as I was then. It's like you are reading some fictional account of a wishful thinking lonely mystic or so. "Right?"

My heart started pounding. I didn't know if I could take it. *How could I travel all the way back home with this beauty at my side?* She was exquisite. "How many times in your life have you sat next to your dream girl?" Literally, "Dream girl?" I mean if I was writing a story it couldn't be more true to what actually occurred.

I decided to play it cool. I was not going to make the initial move, not a single word was going to pass from my lips. She would have to make the first move. She would have to initiate any contact. The initial response was strictly hers. I was aloof, uninterested and appeared unconcerned. I thought about falling asleep or perhaps even changing seats.

It was at that moment that I turned towards her and looked her straight in the eyes and said: "Nice hat," so much for planning.

She smiled and said, "Oh, you must have seen me with it on, outside."

I said, "Yes."

We spoke for quite a bit: Actually, non-stop during the entire trip. We couldn't get enough in. I have absolutely no recollection of anything that we talked about. Imagine hours upon hours of chitchat and not remembering even a single syllable. *How is that possible*?

And then *comes* the "rub" as the Bard used to say. She told me she was married.

In all the years that I have been single and there have been one or two of those, I've never hooked up with a married woman, nor ever intend to. Adultery was not my thing. I was despondent. However, she quickly added that she was looking for a way out and wanted to get a divorce. My heart returned from the depths it had plummeted to as a submerged buoy jumps back up to the water. As we approached the airport, I gave her my phone number.

She lived in Canada and was going to get a connecting flight, but had a seven-hour layover. I told her to call me and we would go for dinner. I was in such major want. My dog Tiger used to pant and breathe heavy when he needed to drink. I saw myself in him at that moment.

We never did have that dinner, or ever spoke again. I had an unusually heavy meditation that afternoon but could swear that I had heard the phone ring. When I came out of it I looked, but I didn't see any messages registered on my answering machine. I knew that it had been her who had called. Perhaps it was for the better. Perhaps it wouldn't have worked out anyway. Perhaps it was a wrong number. Perhaps, perhaps, perhaps.

The City

My head was adorned with my earphones, my feet assumed the fetal position; my ticket was prepared for the conductor and was firmly grasped between my fingers. I just happened to glance up. One at a time, I saw the "priests" walk into my car and sit two seats directly in front of me. Of course, they had been comfortably seated in their previous car. Why they changed cars and followed me several cars up is, of course, one of life's inexplicable mysteries. I stayed in my seat, I was too comfortable.

My mother always told me when three nuns cross her path something unusual usually happens. For her, it was three nuns. For me, it was three priests. Especially now when I looked closer the three "priests" didn't even have collars on, they weren't even wearing turtlenecks? *Very strange. I had seen collars on them earlier? Not to worry* I th ought, at the very least, it would be an interesting evening. I'm seeing things already, and haven't even lit any candles. Who knows what else I might expect, especially after eating some oil-laden *latkes*, which for the uninitiated, are Jewish potato pancakes.

Pop usually picks me up at the station. Sometimes Mom is with him. Tonight he came alone. It's funny how even at a mellow age, I still feel like a kid when I see him. It didn't feel any different when I stretched over to give him a *hello* kiss now, then when I did so as a teenager. Of course, it was no different other than having to fight with the seat belt for more room this time; my waist had grown as a result of affluence and relationships.

Our conversational repertoire was limited. We usually bantered about a few select topics: Stocks, my job, my mom, my debts and my latest "blind dates." I'm the perpetual *dater* in the family. All the years of still being single gave me that noble distinction. I thoroughly enjoyed the moments that I could elicit a smile and even more rare, a laugh from him. For me, humor is the greatest art. It is a high healing and noble art form. To get him to laugh brought joy to my heart and fulfillment to my soul and spirit.

Tonight I was in rare form. I was able to get him to laugh several times. We talked about how his airplane stocks are flying south, his recycling stocks are becoming garbage and his other waste stocks will one day make it big. Hopeful, in this century.

Then the conversation shifted to Mom and before we knew it, we had already arrived at their house.

That night I was exhausted: Exhausted from the week, exhausted from the trip, exhausted from the year and exhausted from exhaustion. I found it difficult to find a comfortable position on that slim pull out bed that had originally belonged to my sibling. It must have been over thirty or forty years old. Little did I know what was ingrained and entrenched in those silent sheets and fluffy pillows, but I was to find out later.

It was as I was drifting out and into sleep, that I started seeing *them*. I thought I was right smack in the middle of a zombie flick. For sure I must have had the TV on and was watching a horror movie. *What I was seeing couldn't have been real?* With eyes closed, I saw them coming through the walls and marching like they were listening to the tune of a distant drum. They weren't walking in line, but they were all walking in the same direction: Forward. There must have been dozens of them: Both men and women. I didn't see any children. They were fully dressed, some in office attire, some in bedtime attire and some were dressed in evening attire. The small room I was in started to feel very close and crowded. They were unaware of me, or if they were they didn't let on that I was present. Their march continued for quite a while, or perhaps even longer because I eventually fell asleep. It appeared as if there were quite a few retired people who hadn't permanently retired yet.

I promised myself this was the last time I would spend a night in that house. I promised myself I would not subject myself to potential ill-health and disease in that manner again. I promised myself many things, but three times afterward, I slept there again and three times afterward, I got sick, again. The fourth time I slept there; I slept upstairs and was no longer subjected to the *Marching Dead*. I suppose, *maybe they didn't like to walk up the stairs?*

I also didn't come down with any illnesses sleeping upstairs since my healing abilities had substantially developed and increased by then, but I did develop a temporary crick in the neck: Sleeping on a narrow couch has its own issues. However, I didn't need calling in the Marker for that.

The things we do for love.

The Sign

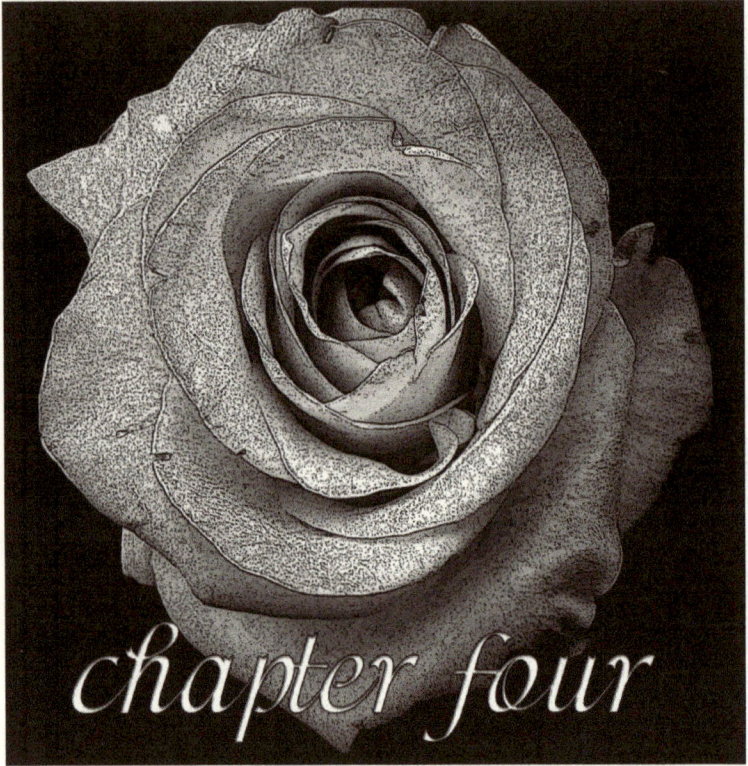

chapter four

Catch it quick,
It may soon be gone.
The obvious is not always
Quickly caught.

God finds ways to show me signs.

Yesterday I was in route to an event to network with people who might turn into potential clients. I had considered going one way and then decided against it, *no let me do it another way.* So I pulled off the road using an exit that was a little bit out of the way, but I felt it was the right route. As I rounded the exit ramp, there it was, bold as day, and quite magnificent. The sky was darkened with storm clouds, but the sun managed to peek out enough to produce a gigantic half rainbow. I can count on one hand how many times I personally have seen them. As I turned the exit and circled it, it was gone: Vanished within seconds. Had I taken the proper exit; I would never have witnessed it. I never would have gotten confirmation I was moving in the right direction. Having gone a bit out of my way to arrive there was worth the results. Sometimes one needs going a bit out of the way to be in the right place at the right time.

Before I began working on my current art project, I wanted to confirm the particular path I had chosen at this point in my life was the right one for me. I had been spending many, many hours using digital image manipulation software on the computer. This was a departure from the usual tools I had previously used to create my art with. Up until then, traditional medias such as inks, pastels, and paints of various types were my chosen tool. As I have previously done from time to time, I asked for confirmation that I was on the right road. I mentally asked for a clear, unmistakable "sign" that I was moving in the right direction. God can hear your thoughts very clearly. I didn't dwell on it and went about my usual way. In other words, I put it out there and continued about my business.

There have been other times that signs have occurred. Several times as a matter of fact, I could be walking on a road, and a hawk's feather comes fluttering down landing right by my foot. As I've gotten older, I've found the time between asking for the sign and it actually occurring has decreased. This time I didn't have to wait long for the response either, although it did catch me totally off guard and much by surprise.

My first car was a coupe. I had wanted a motorcycle, but luckily, Mom put her foot down and insisted I get a car instead. Given my history with bikes, as you shall read in *The Parrot*, she most probably saved my life with this denial. So as a high school graduation present, they bought me a coupe. I believe it cost $1000.00; it was used or as they now say, a certified pre-owned vehicle. Way back then in the old days, it was just a used car. It was a hot car. It was my pride and joy. You can only imagine a curly haired young kid in a high school jacket with white leather arms riding around in a cool blue car, which is now iconic. It was a sight to behold. I loved that car. I loved storing my high school jacket in the trunk for safekeeping. At the time, these were two of my most prized possessions.

Mom did right by canceling the motorbike idea. This was way much better. Dad did right by picking it. He knew about cars and engines. He taught me how to drive it, how to take out the spark plugs, gap them or replace them and how to change the carburetor. At that time cars were simple. They were tinker-able. They were fun. All you needed was a good wrench, some muscles, and some know-how. And surprisingly they were also fast, fast and fast. I never had any issues with it, while I had it. It was safe. That one time I almost went over the Brooklyn Bridge with it never happened, because power steering didn't exist in that car. I was able to avert what might have been a pretty big accident with a few simple, intuitive maneuvers.

My biggest issue was parking. Street parking can be tough. Having to move the car daily from side to side was a pain, but *no pain no gain*, "Right?" Pop didn't like it either. When I took off for the summer, (my second graduation present) and toured about overseas, he was stuck with having to move the car around. Although he complained about it afterward, I suspect he didn't mind it too much; after all, it was a cool, cool car. I remember once coming out of the movie theater after having seen a film that had my car in it. The parents were both in the back seat of the car, I was playing chauffeur. I looked around to see if there were any cars coming in both directions. Of course, the car was a manual stick shift. I revved the engine and popped the clutch and the car tore out of the parking spot, as it did in the movie. Mom started screaming at me. Pop just smiled. I loved that car.

I even had it repainted. At that time you could do anything for almost nothing. I think it was under $50.00 to have it painted metallic blue. It was beautiful, to begin with, but having it in metallic blue was over-the-top.

It must have stood out like a sore thumb on the streets of the residentially zoned neighborhood. Not too many cars of that type adorned the neighborhood. Pop's car occupied the garage, so mine was outsourced to street parking. When I came back from my trip, moving the car was my responsibility again. There were three spots I always used to park the car in on my block. It was a family block where everyone knew each other. *Who would have suspected?*

I woke up on a Sunday morning, showered and dressed as usual. I was still living at home then. I didn't move out until later that year. I walked over to the kitchen window and looked out to take a look at my pride and joy. You know the feeling: The one where the world just fell out from under your feet: The one where that sinking feeling in the pit of your stomach keeps getting deeper and deeper. Your mouth turns dry and all that heat that rushes up to your cheeks and overpowers any semblance of control you have over your body. At first, you have to pee, then you need to have a drink because your mouth is so dry you can't even swallow.

Pop noticed it first and asked me, "What's wrong?"

I looked at him. *I didn't know what to say?*

He asked again, "What's wrong?"

I went to the window and while looking out I said to him, "It's gone."

He knew what I was saying and said, "Why don't you go for a walk around the block. Maybe you parked it somewhere else last night."

As an exercise in futility, I went out to look. Nowadays I might forget where I parked my car. Nowadays, I might forget I had a car, but then, I was sharp as a blade and quick as a bullet. No memory lapse or loss for me. I did as Pop said, and walked around the block knowing full well that my baby was gone, gone, gone.

Of course, there was no coupe parked anywhere around the block. Of course, the car had been stolen. My electric-blue hot rod was hot-roding somewhere else. To make matters even worse, my high school jacket was in the trunk of the car. Double whammy, double worse: Major trauma for a teenager.

Pop and I went to the police station. We filled out the necessary paperwork. On the way out, the detective shouted to us, "By the way, if you find it, please let us know." I looked at Pop and he at me. He just motioned with his right hand upwards and to the right. The one that says, "What can I say, it just is the way it is."

It's been a few years now, and I still haven't called that detective. You are not surprised. "Right?"

I've had cool cars. Cars I've kept and a car I've totaled, not intentionally of course. I would say the car I had at present was as much a classic dream car now as the coupe was then. It was also a coupe. But what made it even more of a dream was that it was a convertible coupe. It was a classic. When I eventually turned it in at the end of the lease, after three years, I had only eight thousand miles on it. Imagine, eight thousand miles. These days I can put eight thousand miles on my muscle car in two months.

Yes, I still love these babies. Even Mom loved it and the picture I took of her in front of it. I blew it up to mural size. It still adorns her basement wall. I could have kept it, but the car was defective. It had a bad engine that stunk. They kept telling me it was this or that. Imagine putting the top down and smelling burnt something in your nostrils. It looked sharp, but it also smelled sharp, acrid to be exact. I wasn't too upset to turn it in. The dealer must have thought I was crazy to do so. I could have bought it and sold it for more. But that was not my way. While I had it, it was still my pride and joy. I even had the opportunity of having a beautiful woman in the front passenger seat. I managed to drive around with the top down and her long blonde hair fluttering in the wind. Some dreams come true. However, that dream lasted as dreams sometimes do, only one night. The memory will be there longer. If you want to catch eternity, do anything. It will always be there. That memory lasts forever.

It was now Sunday and as most Sundays go, I called the garage to bring my *toy car* up so I could take it for a spin downtown. That is where I usually went for brunch on the weekends. I had a favorite restaurant and usually parked the car in the same place at the same time each Sunday. One might call it a ritual of sorts. This time my car was the only one on that block. *Strange* I thought. I looked around to see if there were any "no parking police signs" or "parade notices" posted. There were none to be found, anywhere.

Coincidence I thought. I found an empty table that just happened to be facing towards the street where my car was parked. I ordered and was waiting on the slow service I was receiving when I notice a large truck with a huge beam on top of it pull along side of my car. The food finally came, it must have been two months after I had ordered it, but I finally started to eat. I was quite hungry.

I happened to glance out again and this time another large truck exactly the same as the first one pulled up in front of my car and secured itself in place. By now the first one had also secured itself in place. My car was blocked in, front and back. Saying I was a tad bit nervous was a considerable understatement. I sprinted out of the restaurant and went over to what looked like the leader of the group who was supervising the raising of several beams towards a huge, empty black cinder block wall on the side of a building directly behind my car.

"Sir, this is my car? Do I need to move it?"

"Don't worry. We aren't going to be here long, but if you want to move your car then we can easily move the trucks and let you get out."

I stood there with my jaw dropped, and mouth wide open.

He continued: "Rest assured that even with the heavy telescoping beams protruding out over your car, your car is very safe."

Sure. I said to myself, *Hey, it was insured. There was even gap insurance on it. If something happened, maybe I could get a car that didn't stink?*

He said they were putting up a sign on the side of the building. I had no clue as to what kind of sign they were putting up and didn't even ask. I went back to brunch since my food was getting cold. Of course, every second was now focused on the coming moment when the rolled up sign would drop. I got so distracted by the waitress who had brought me my check that I didn't even witness the unveiling of the sign. Sometimes it appears as if something conspires against things going as you planned, allowing some significant events to unravel themselves when you aren't looking.

When I had finished paying the check, I looked up and there was a huge canvas, several billboards high in size, suspended over the entire side of the building. This canvas billboard was advertising the specific branded software that I was using for the series of digital paintings I was now creating.

It wasn't until several hours later that I realized the full implications of what had just occurred. Yes, sometimes, the cool coupe kid is slow, slow, slow. I had just received a clear, unmistakable *sign* that I was moving in the right direction. I was pleased. I had gotten my confirmation. I continued with the creation of the current series, which I was working on. All though I didn't know it at the time, the completed digital paintings are ones that I used to later illustrate future books and music albums.

I entered my convertible coupe still thinking about my first car...

The Cow

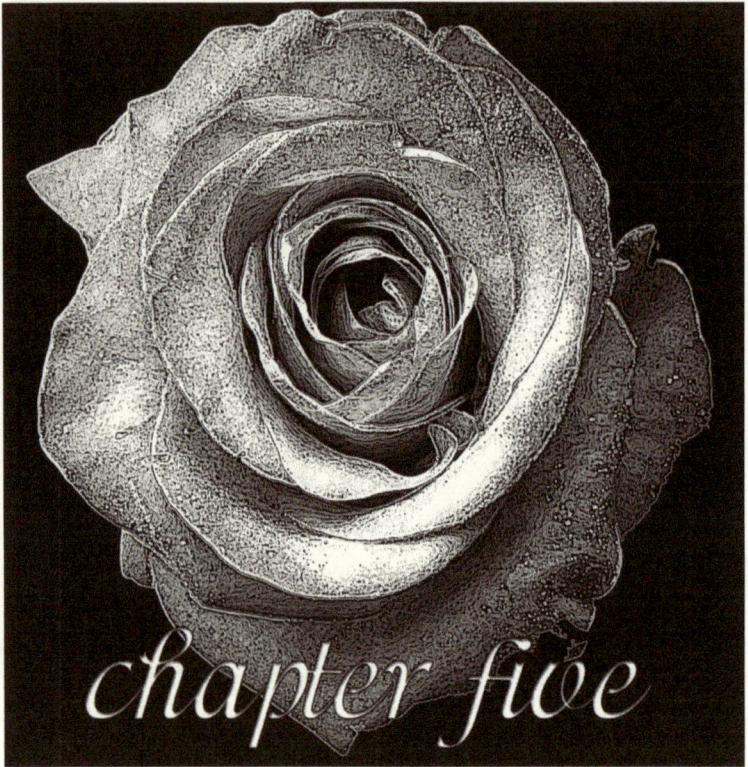

chapter five

When all is lost,
Something may be found.
Sometimes what jingles
Is a familiar sound.

I've had an attraction to and fascinations with the paranormal as well as spirituality since early on in life. On that night it sat right next to me, under the guise of my grandmother.

I had just received my high school graduation present, a '65 baby blue, stick shift coupe. (You previously met her.) I was entering college in the fall. My hair was greased, my arms covered with a white leather and cotton high school jacket, which proudly displayed my school's tennis team emblem. A picture of the times: Clean-cut, preppy and ready to roll. This was a sharp juxtaposition to the cultural, environment which surrounded my family life. The summer was going to provide me with my first experience of living away from my parent. My grandparents were going abroad and had given me permission to use their apartment while they were away.

My grandmother had called me to come to pick her up and drive her to my house. My grandparents lived about twenty minutes from my parent's house. It happened to be a tumultuous spring night, with thunderstorms and torrential rains. It became dark early that evening, not because the sun went down, but because of the clouds, which were filled with blackness. It was a perfect night for a ghost story.

My grandmother was born in Poland and was a Holocaust survivor. Even now, she still only spoke a few words of English.

As I was growing up, she taught me how to speak her language in order for us to be able to communicate. She taught me Yiddish, which to this day I speak fluently, but sadly too infrequently. It is quite musical and colorful a language as well as being sonically emphatic. I have been bilingual since childhood.

I pulled up to her house, revved up my new horses, shut her down and bopped up to get her. Of course, she was happy to see me and was more talkative than usual. Her life was that of a housewife and her stories were those of the experiences she had lived through during the war. Tonight she told me a new one. A story neither the rest of my close cousins nor I would soon forget.

At her funeral last year, it was a story that was retold as a family heirloom. It was not a fabrication of her imagination. It was a slice of reality not often glimpsed by most, but then again during exceptional times, exceptional experiences can occur. Her stories and those of my grandfather were filled with tales of *miraculous* survivals and divine interventions. They were almost enough to prompt belief in a higher being.

As was her usual manner, she started with several incidents of escape. With hindsight, I now realize she was testing me to see how far she could go. She was fishing to see if she could tell me that really big one. She wanted to see if it would frighten me or perhaps make me think she had lost it. The Babeh, as I called her, she had many names, was many things, but for sure, one thing that she was not was *out there*. The sign of *losing it* in our family was placing your handbag in the refrigerator. This was not something she ever did.

She was my mother's mother. On my father's side, the entire family less two uncles died in the Holocaust. The only contact I've had with that side has been through mediums who have channeled them for me. One of the live uncles I was able to meet. He lived in Israel, the other lived in Russia and I never connected with him.

So, as one of the largest flashes of lightning lit up the evening sky and perhaps the loudest thunderclap I had ever heard broke loose, she began her tale. The torrential rain was pelting against the windshield and thundering upon the roof of my car. She told me her story in Yiddish, and I translate it here for you to the best of my memory.

The Cow

It became increasingly clear to her that it was necessary to pick up whatever clothing she could carry as well as her three youngest children. They were about seven, eight and ten years old. With packs on their backs, in unison, they all began running. It was September 1, 1939. There were loud rumors that the Germans were coming to collect the Jews. It was night and she found herself heavy burdened with bundles and screaming children in the middle of a barren field. That was when it started.

The skies became ablaze with fire and the sound of thundering bombs circling the field was deafening. The thunderstorm that night in Brooklyn most probably triggered these memories.

The blazing circle of flames started to inch ever-closer inward to where all four lay crumpled, huddled and pressed into the ground. She covered the children with the bundles she had carried. Their wailing could be heard above the sound of dropping bombs. It was becoming increasingly evident that *there was no escape.* She too began crying. Being the reverent, religious, and pious soul that she was, she entreated the Divinity for immediate assistance: Right then and there.

After several moments, hours or days, time ceases at times like that, she felt a tap on her shoulder. At first, she ignored it. She knew there was no one there, but it persisted. When she stopped sobbing and began to turn to see who was there, a masculine voice told her not to turn up or look around, but just to listen to what was being said to her. She told me at first she was stunned but was happy that someone was there to help her. She did think it a bit unusual that she was being told not to turn around, but she listened anyway. *What choice did she have?*

The voice told her to put the children on the cow, and the cow would lead her and them out of the field to safety. At that point, she couldn't resist turning around. It was more a reflex action. She had to look. She turned. There was no one behind her. No one was there, but something was. Standing directly behind, there stood a cow. It was calmly looking right at her. An embroidered bridle was around its neck. She hadn't noticed a cow in the field previously. The field had been barren. *There was no place it could have come from.* She didn't have time to think. She grabbed the children and placed them on the cow's back. She then piled her bundles on it too and took hold of the bridle. The cow, as placid as it was moments ago, swiftly began to forge a path toward the fire at one end of the field.

From where she stood, it looked like it was going to lead all of them into the flames, but there was something familiar about the voice that had spoken to her moments ago and there was something familiar about that hand that had quickly, yet intensely rested itself upon her left shoulder. She trusted that voice. She felt a warmth from that hand. She followed the cow.

As the cow approached what looked like a firewall, as it moved towards a seemingly solid impasse of flames, there appeared a break in the flames. As if a hidden breath had paved a path through the dense flames. Smoke profusely filled the air. She closed her eyes and allowed herself to be led by the cow. All that she could hear was the sound of a bell tinkling from its bridle. The sounds of the bombs falling, the sounds of the grasses crackling and the sounds of the children screaming were all muted by the tinkling of that bell. She had heard that sound before. Like the voice, and like that hand she knew those tinkles.

It only took a few brief moments that seemed longer than an eternity for her before the cow stopped. She looked around. She, the children, her bundles and the cow were now safe. They found themselves in the cabbage patch, which surrounded the field.

She lifted the children off the cow and then did the same for the bundles. By now the children had stopped crying. She fell to her knees and started to pray, thanking the Almighty, as she was fond of calling him, for their salvation. It was then that she remembered. She remembered that voice, she remembered that hand, and she remembered that cow. She remembered how she had always loved her grandfather. How she had loved visiting him at his farm. She remembered how she had loved drinking the fresh milk and playing with the bells. She remembered how his hand had always felt warm and strong and firm when he rested it upon her shoulder. She remembered how he had always loved her. She now remembered who had spoken to her and now remembered to whom that cow belonged. She thought to herself that for sure it was he who had helped her and for sure it was his cow. It even had the same bridle and bell hanging from its neck. Once again she turned to look for sure. Once again as it was there when it was, it now wasn't there where it once was. The cow was gone.

Most probably with the same motivation as my father had had that night in the synagogue when we discussed God, she asked me not to repeat the story, but assured me it was quite true.

My cousin and his father, my uncle, her son and one of the three children that experienced that night went to Poland this past summer. To visit their past and they went to the very field where this had occurred. It existed exactly as described. Perhaps they thought they too would hear a tinkle of a bell and feel a hand pressed upon their shoulder. But for them, it was enough to know that the story was truly a reality. I never needed to put it to the test.

Bells were not the only thing I was going to hear.

Surprisingly, even upon passing the *Babeh* was able to bring the cow back for a cameo. The first time she came through for me during a psychic reading. The medium said, "I don't know why, but a short, gray-haired, and elderly woman, who I believe is your grandmother on your mother's side, has just walked into the room. She is holding an embroidered bridle that's attached to a cow that is trailing behind her? She wants you to know she is all right and has come to say, 'Hello.' " I'm sure had I listened carefully, I would have heard a tinkling bell.

Much to my surprise at her funeral, another one of my cousins recited the "Story of the Cow" to all present. I later found out that all though she had asked me not to repeat it; apparently she had asked several others also not to repeat it. I wasn't the only one, she had told it to, but I was the only one at the first funeral I ever attended to experience the events that transpired on that day.

The Funeral

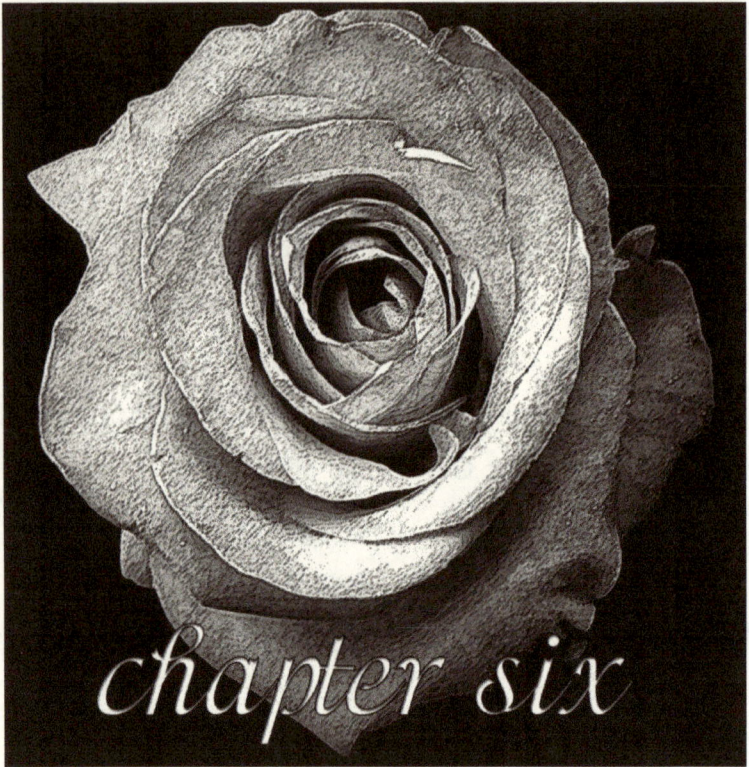

chapter six

*Not all
That you see
Is seen by all
That see you.*

For security purposes, some hi-value establishments have two consecutive entrance doors, which can only open one at a time. This way there is never a clear path in or out of the premises. This prevents unauthorized entry into the premises but does not prevent unusual occurrences from happening outside of the premises.

It was in the middle of a harsh winter, and the snowfall was plentiful. Last winter was a much milder one. I hardly had to shovel. This winter I had to shovel quite often, and this was a stormy day. I had never attended a funeral, although death had crossed my path once before. Much to my disappointment, circumstances, which were not under my control prevented me from being able to attend that funeral of Zen Ben.

At that time I was studying at a College of Oriental Medicine in Asia. I had been living there for not more than three months when I received a letter. The outside of the envelope had "NUMBER 3" written in bold red letters on its lower left-hand side. I thought *perhaps it was part of a series of letters sent from home?* It did seem strange to be getting number three before receiving the other two first. I always enjoyed reconnecting with my family back home and at present, these letters were the only way of doing so. I would have had to take a three-hour bus ride to the capital city of the country I was in if I wanted to make a phone call to the states. I lived in a very rural area.

Sometimes you know when you shouldn't do anything before you do something. I knew I should have waited until the mail came tomorrow, or perhaps even a day after that. *What was the rush?* It was not like the envelope was disappearing anytime soon. *I should ha', should ha', should ha'.* I didn't. I opened it anyway. I should ha' waited.

It began with: "And so Zidda passed away." Zidda is Yiddish for grandfather.

Several days later I received NUMBERS "1" & "2", but by that time I had almost boarded a plane to return to the states for the funeral. Via a trip to the city to make the phone call, I found out that the funeral had already taken place three weeks earlier. The family had purposely waited to tell me about what had occurred given the strong likelihood that I would be prompted to return and interrupt my studies. What a hard decision it must have been for the family not to immediately tell me. Especially since they knew of the closeness, I had enjoyed sharing with my Ziddeh.

Mourning was a difficult experience for me. I had never observed the ritual before, so it was new to me. Being in a faraway place absent of family, there was no ritual. No customary seven days of "Shiva." No solace, no hugs, no tears, and no comfort. There was no one to share my grief with. When I finally brought myself to call and connect with those dearest to me, I had already attained a level of composure. I didn't want to speak to them with me needing their comfort; I wanted to be there for them.

I never got to see *Zen Ben* as I used to call him, the husband of *Hitou* as I called her, who was my grandmother from *The Cow*, buried. But I suppose that was what he wanted it to be. When I saw him for that last time at the airport. When I looked at his face and saw the color of his nose, I knew he would not be here too much longer. I was trained and skilled in the ancient art of reading faces even then. One could see and know quite a bit about a person from their face and their eyes. When I said goodbye, that time—I really did say, "Goodbye." And so I remember him always as being alive since I really never witnessed his death. It was at another funeral that I was to encounter the exact opposite.

The Visitor

Fortunately, my Pop was still alive at the initial time of this writing. My friend had just lost his. Paul was the only son of a Swiss family that owned a business located in Long Island. He was a few years younger, had a lot more hair, and was also much shorter than me. He did a good job of learning the business of running his father's business. He was too busy working all the time to start a family; much to his father's regret. I had transacted some business with Paul a few years ago and had often kept in touch. I suppose he looked at me as the older brother he never had. He felt quite close to me.

It was not surprising that when his father passed, he asked if I would be his companion for the day. I knew he didn't have too many friends. In this respect, we were similar. As was customary in Jewish religion the mourner, the one who had lost a parent was not supposed to be left alone on the day of the funeral. It was my responsibility to be his companion for the entire day. I almost fulfilled this duty in its entirety: The key word, of course, being *entirety*.

My friend insisted upon coming to work prior to going to the funeral. It was a busy day at his office, constant condolence phone calls. I had taken the day off and was hanging out in his office with him. The time to leave was fast approaching, and I kept hurrying him to get off the phone and get going. Finally, he agreed and we began to depart, heading towards the two exit doors. We opened the first, and I stepped into the small corridor between the two doors with him following directly behind me. But, before the door shut he ran out of the passageway yelling that he had forgotten his cell phone. He rushed back to get it.

The door shut and he was back in the office, without me. I couldn't go back in and had to exit through the other door since the inner door was already securely locked. I had failed my mission: Not to leave him alone for even one minute. *Not good* I thought.

The lobby of the office was glass enclosed. Suzy, the receptionist could clearly see the entire lobby from where she sat. As I exited the outer door, I motioned to her to buzz me back in. You had to be buzzed back in order to gain entrance. When I turned around to re-enter, I was surprised to see an old man waiting in front of the elevator door.

He approached and in a heavy Swiss accent asked, "Are you going to the funeral?"

I said, "Yes" and was going to ask if he was coming with us, I assumed he was a relative when I saw Suzy waving frantically for me to quickly come back into the office. I told him that I would be right back. He just nodded. Suzy buzzed me in, and I went into the office to see where my friend was and what the receptionist wanted.

When I walked in Suzy told me that my friend had to take an important phone call from overseas, his Aunt had just heard about her brother. I went into his office. By then he had finished the call. We both went out through both of the doors, this time together. I was expecting to see the old man waiting in the lobby, but no one was there. I had a feeling not to mention the man to my friend, so I didn't.

As we were walking out of the lobby, I asked the Herbert, the security guard if he had allowed anyone to come up to the floor. Herbert was an ex-marine and a retired police officer. He would have noticed if someone had wanted to come up. He said, "No." So as they say, "The plot thickens," pun not intended.

When we arrived at the funeral parlor, I was expecting to see the old man there, after all, he had asked if I was going to the funeral. I looked at everyone present. No one even resembled him. I thought *perhaps he got stuck in traffic?* The whole incident actually drifted out of my mind during the course of the day. I didn't see him at the actual funeral either.

Later that night, I went to the house of the deceased to pay a Shiva call. Shiva is seven days of mourning for the dead. It is a time when family and friends come to comfort those who are grieving. As I mentioned, it was something that I had not been able to do when my grandfather passed and this was the first time that I had attended one.

It is customary in the Jewish religion to cover all mirrors and to turn over or cover all pictures of the deceased so as not to cause further discomfort for the mourners. I never followed rules; it is still hard for me to do so. When no one was looking, I turned over one of the pictures to see what Paul's father had looked like since I had never met him. I know it was something I should never have done. It wasn't my house, and I was breaking the rules. "What can I say? Guilty as charged." But you are right. I never should 'ha done it.

I suppose by now you've guessed whose face I saw on that photo.

I never told my friend about it. The next day I went over to my friend's office. He wasn't there; he was out for a week. I wanted to bring closure to the experience that I had yesterday. I asked the receptionist, Suzy, the one that had called for me to come back into the office, the one that was looking directly at me and the old man since he was standing right next to me in the lobby. In a coyish way, I said, "Were there any visitors on the day of the funeral, other than me?" I didn't want to directly ask her if she had seen the old man standing right next to me.

This was her response: "You know, funny that you ask that. I was very surprised that no one came over here to go to the funeral with you and Paul."

She had never seen the old man and I never saw him again, either.

The Gift

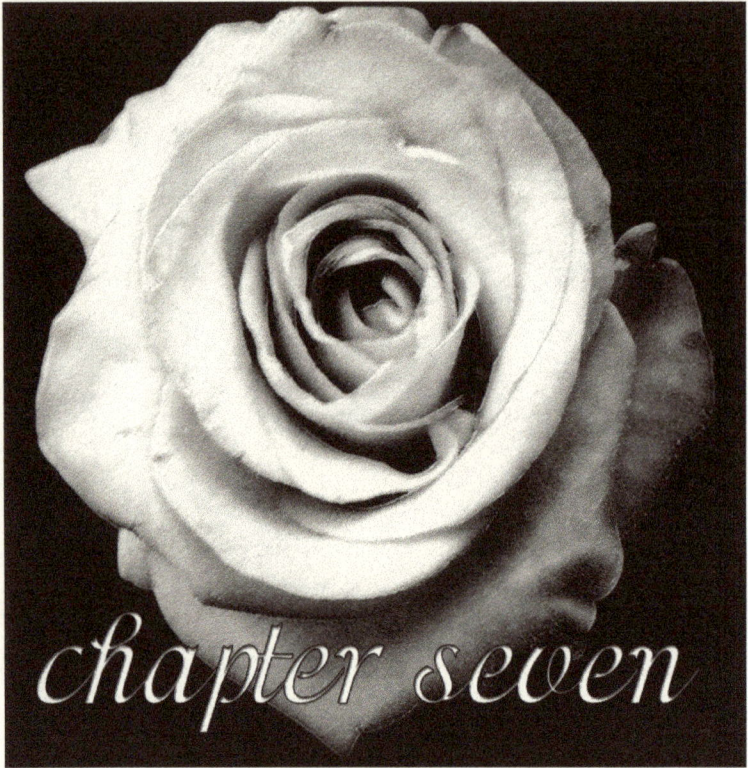

chapter seven

Oh, lint I may,
Oh, lint I might,
Have you vanished,
From my sight.

God always finds ways to show me love.

I like wearing red, white and black clothes around Christmas time. Not because I think I'm Santa, but because these colors vibrate to frequencies that harmonize with the energies present at those times. Wearing these colors allows me to tune in to them, or at least I think so. Of course, the most common example is wearing green on Saint Patrick's Day. Another one is the orange of Thanksgiving Day or the explosive red, white and blue for the Fourth of July.

I enjoy wearing fine clothes, as well as shopping for them. Roaming around in a department store, a mall or on the NYC avenues is a euphoric diversion. Although I can only handle it for less than an hour at a time, still it allows my often too focused being to let loose.

There are billions of people on the planet, but only three thought of me for the holidays this year. I would be thankful for even only one, let alone three. Some have none. The first was Mom.

Gift One

Mom doesn't really go out and buy me a present, although on occasion she has done so: A metal can of chocolate popcorn and some dishtowels, to mention only a few. That tin might as well have been cast in platinum. That's how precious it is to me. Not that she doesn't have an excellent fashion sense; she happens to have one, but more so, she doesn't have access or opportunity to purchase current avant-garde fashion as I do. She also can't afford to pay what I pay for my clothes. We have an unwritten custom of me finding something special for myself and then her contributing a very small portion towards its cost: $1.00 or perhaps $5.00, never more.

This year it was a beautiful red, fitted, fleece, and zippered high collared jacket. It was soon destined to become my second skin during the upcoming winter. It had a multitude of zippered pockets and felt incredible on. It made me look slimmer than I was and kept me quite comfortable even in very cold country weather. I had called her right after I brought it home and informed her of the gift that she had gotten for me. After the call, I sent her a multimedia picture message of me wearing it. It took quite a while, but I was able to teach my aged, immigrant mom how to text and picture message. She was also digital camera and photo printer savvy too, I was proud of her. When I came to her house to pack her up for the annual hibernation to Florida, she graciously handed me a dollar bill for my first present. Years later, I was devastated when I happened to burn the sleeve of the jacket one winter. I was baking bread (my new passion) when the sleeve touched the inside of the oven. The jacket had saved me from a very nasty burn; however, my sleeve now had a burned spot on it. I thought it would have to be pitched.

Mom loved doi ng her nails; she was quite good at applying little flowers to them. When I went visiting one Sunday, I saw her sitting at the kitchen table doing her nails with flowers and the thought immediately occurred: *Put an embroidered flower on the sleeve of her present to cover up the burn.* I was pleased with myself and that my prized article of clothing was to be resurrected. We both picked the appliqué together. It read, "Mom," and had a rose next to it. I left the jacket with her, and she had the appliqué sewed on. We were both pleased. I now wore a flowered "Mom" upon my sleeve. My second present occurred at the office.

Gift Two

There hasn't been a significant other in my life for a while now. The closest thing to a relationship I've had was a casual smile and hello from someone in the building that I work in. You can always tell when someone cares for you in a more than just platonic way. Their smile is a bit more curved and prolonged, their voice is a tad bit sweeter, and they always find excuses to stand closer to you so that the scent of their perfume wafts nearer to your person. Sometimes they even secretly gaze at you while passing by and go so far as to give you a card and a gift on the holidays. Her name was Louise. She was about six inches taller than me.

I've had a passion for collecting pens for a while now. Perhaps, because life has been good and I've had the means to enjoy doing so. Those at the office knew that about me, as did the sales people at the stationery shop located in the building where I worked. Louise was a salesperson there. I suppose that hope always runs eternal for those that have passion, but some things are not meant to be despite the attraction and desire. For me there were always trigger points for such, not that I differ much from the rest of my gender, I suspect. She struck some of them. But there have also been flags that get waived upon learning things about the intended paramour.

I've found that as one gets older, one learns to be able to resist that which wouldn't work out before one even engages in a relationship to discover it wouldn't work out. Possibly, youth has a greater openness to compromise with and adapt to conditions, which might have been present had a relationship been pursued. At the point in life, I currently found myself in, my consciously intended directions, or as of yet unknown ones, prompted me to hold fast to the path that I was pursuing without needing to be sidetracked. Earlier in life, I got sidetracked easily and often. Now I held to my own.

I also suspect some could make an argument for allowing themselves to participate in the experience and not eclipse events a priori due to an ability, which enabled their vision to see a probable outcome well in advance. After all, if one's vision is astute and premonitory enough to see far into the future, *doesn't it behoove one to abide by such discerning and discriminating revelations?* Or perhaps, *one should take the approach of throwing caution to the wind and indulge in a highly exciting, but ultimately doomed encounter?* Much to the chagrin of my baser parts, I opted for the platonic stance in spite of viscerally lusting for a different approach.

Thus, once a year via a subdued gift card, which was shrouded in veiled tautology, Louise proclaimed semblances of feelings and gave me a gift of a pen.

A pen can be a very personal item. I did not need to be constantly reminded of a relationship which wasn't going to be. I farmed out the pens, which I received from her to those who I loved as gifts for the holidays. In this instance, *Out of sight, out of mind* worked best for me. I had to remind myself that sometimes danger may lurk beneath calm, serene, inviting, but highly deceptive waters. Over time I found that in spite of what evidence was presented, I needed to go by my gut. It saw much farther into the future than immediately observable phenomena.

My pen collection was not receiving another addition this year. Of course, a pen aficionado never had enough pens, just as a car addict never has enough cars. I now realize it is a sickness. Given all the things one can do with discretionary income, overindulgence is ludicrous, however, at the time, I thought it a luxury and perk.

I decided to send it off to Mom as a holiday gift along with some DVDs. I like keeping her entertained. I packed them and the pen carefully and shipped both out to her. Interestingly enough, and without any plausible and logical explanation, the pen arrived completely broken. It was still secured in its box but snapped right in half at the stem.

"So what do you think? Was it perhaps cabin pressure, or maybe, the projected wrath of a woman's scorn?" I had my suspicions, and I leave you to yours…

Gift Three

I wanted to wear my new red jacket to the office on the day we were to close for vacation. It would be my Santa suit. However, I needed to have a white shirt and black slacks to make up the true power color outfit. I kept a mandarin-collared white shirt in tip-top shape just for such an occasion. It was different looking. I've found that this style of shirt can't easily be purchased when you needed it.

Like many, I enjoy wearing corduroy pants in the winter, and I am partial to designer labels. So, a pair black corduroy, designer slacks was a perfect accouterment to my Santa outfit on the last day of work of the old year. I get the week between Christmas, and New Year's off for vacation. I tried the pants on. They were perfect, except for two things: The first of which was their fit. It feels good putting on clothes that feel big on you, which in this case felt huge on me. Of course, it also feels good putting on clothes that fit perfectly. But next to that, clothes that feel big on you feel much better than trying on clothes that feel too small. Those make you feel fat. The former was the case for me.

The waist wrapped around and overlapped my belt. I had dropped about twenty-five pounds from the last holiday and these pants clearly attested to that fact. I smiled. I decided that in spite of the fit, I was going to proudly wear them as a personal "badge of courage," which of course, in this case, wasn't red. But there was one small and minor detail, or in this case, a whole host of minor details which personified themselves into a multitude of white specs: *Lint.* I wasn't going to allow small specs of discarded nothingness to deter me from my planned outfit. and I was determined to remedy the unexpected kink in my plans promptly.

I tried making several mental notes to myself to purchase a lint brush on the way home from work that night. The memory isn't what it used to be, so I even emailed myself a to-do list to remind me to do so. Emailing myself works better than a to-do list. I would somehow have to somewhere write down that I should look at my to-do list to do it. Since I didn't look at my to-do list that often, even if I had written down to look at it, I wouldn't have seen that task because I wasn't checking for it in the first place. I know this is another one of the great cosmic mysteries like the chicken and the egg.

I arrived at work on the day before I was planning to dress like a Santa, very excited about my intended new outfit for tomorrow. The year's end is usually busy. Everyone rushes to get their work done before vacation. I was especially busy too and left quite late. I hadn't slept well the night before, had a light dinner and then went straight to sleep. I didn't even look at any emails, let alone review my non-existent to-do list.

I awoke the next morning excited about my last day at work before vacation, showered and started to get dressed. Then it hit me! I had forgotten to buy the lint brush. I was still determined to play Santa, so I dressed as planned, lint or not. I took a cab to work because I didn't want the fashion police to see me wearing linty pants. I figured I would run out and find a lint brush after opening the office up.

I opened up, checked my email, which was now repeatedly reminding me to go and buy a lint brush and started to get up to leave my office. As I started proceeding out, I heard a knock at my office door.

I acknowledged whoever was knocking to come in. One of the people that I supervise came in with a wrapped item in their hand. She wasn't someone that I had a close relationship with at the office. I hardly even knew her. She was a new hire with very little experience. She must have thought it was required to give her supervisor a gift for the holidays. She walked over to me, and with a great big smile she wished me a happy holiday and handed me her Christmas present. I was happy to receive the gift and humbly thanked her. She left, and I closed the door behind her. I eagerly sat down and began unwrapping my present. I wanted to leave it lying on my desk unopened until I came back with the lint brush, but the child in me wouldn't let that happen. That child quickly ripped open the gift-wrap. I almost fell off from my chair when I saw what was under those wrappings.

There in my hands was an oversized, giant lint brush. I cut open the plastic shell surrounding it. I started unraveling its outer wrap when I noticed the logo on the tape, which the lint brush was wrapped with: It was a smiling angel. I had received my third gift.

God is not only good, but also very clean! Happy Holidays!

The Parrot

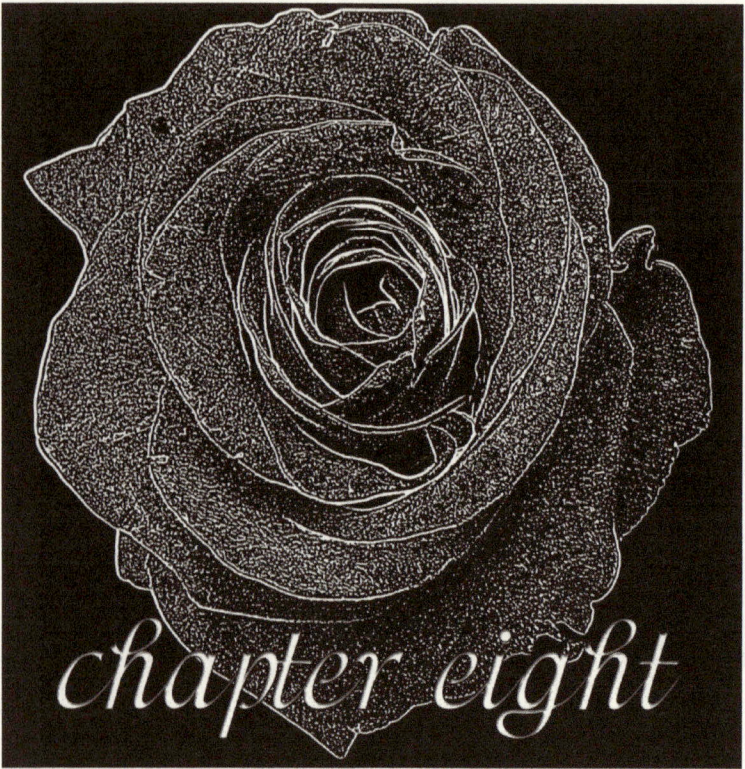

chapter eight

Polly doesn't always
Want a cracker,
Sometimes she likes
Finger food.

My father passed on the day before Rosh Hashanah.

It is said to be a blessed day to die. I will always remember which day he died on, because of that. He made it easy for us to remember. Of course, most would say, "No day is a good day to die,' but the solemnity and spirituality that precedes and encompasses the Jewish High Holy days gave his passing a greater degree of importance, respect and more importantly, his dying on that particular day allowed us to be able to sit a full Shiva schedule. Jewish people mourn for seven days unless a holiday interrupts this schedule. The day he died was the last day he could have died on that would allow his family to mourn a full seven days at that time of the year. It was a good day to die on.

Subsequently, and on several occasions thereafter, he has appeared to me in dreams as a vehicle for communicating information to me. The first time was the day after he had died, a story I will save. Last night was another time.

Age sometimes wakes us in the night or with me early in the morning if I happen to indulge myself with a small bottle of flavored seltzer. I don't drink just any flavored seltzer since there is a dramatic difference between seltzer from a glass bottle and seltzer from a plastic one. From a glass bottle, you can feel the firm, hard, coolness without the *plasticy* aftertaste. 5:00 a.m. often calls to me. This is both good and bad: Bad because I like being completely asleep. I have enough to deal with during the day that I don't need subconscious or superconscious awareness' during sleep rearing their heads up at me. However, of late it looks like I still have tales to tell and am not quite ready to retire and sit on my bench staring at nothing. So the dream that I just had was quite clear. When I arose and walked to the bathroom, I remembered it quite vividly.

I don't open my eyes when I head for the John in the middle of the night. I keep them closed and feel my way around. I rationalize that in this way I can go back to sleep quicker. Sometimes it works and one time it didn't. I walked right smack into the door and greeted it with my left brow and eye. I was fortunate. I was even able to go back to sleep afterward. But that incident did not deter me from still keeping my eyes closed. It even appears that "near corner mishaps" are a family trait.

A few months ago when Mom was visiting at the house, she almost walked into the corner of my hallway/kitchen wall. She swears that an invisible, but dark shadow materialized between her and the wall and physically prevented her from banging into the wall. I'll save that one too because I started telling you about the parrot I saw last night in a dream, so I will stay on track and not *fly the coup*.

The Dream

My father led me into an unused portion of an unfamiliar house. He looked like he had looked when he was in his 30's. He opened the door, and we both walked into a dark, dusty room, which was cluttered and had a large, cube-shaped object off to one of its sides. It was covered with a bundled hopsack cloth around it. He picked both up and placed them on a nearby table, dusting the table with his breath before he put the covered, cube-shaped object down upon it. When he unraveled the wrappings, I could see a beautiful, multicolored parrot standing on a perch within the metal cage. The cage was one that I remember having seen before.

Without looking at me, he opened the latch of the cage door and reached inside to offer his downturned hand as a perch for what appeared to be a huge multicolored macaw. The bird lunged for his hand twice. Given the angle, I couldn't see if the bird had nipped him, or not.

So I asked, "Did the bird get you?"

He answered, "Not the second time."

He reached in farther, and the bird allowed itself to be removed from its habitat. There was a wheelchair nearby, and he asked me to sit on it. He then placed the bird on my shoulder, the right one vs. the left one. Once the parrot was on me, I realized why he had asked me to sit on the chair: The bird was enormously heavy. Strangely, this weight dissipated quickly and the bird turned to me and said, "Let's play ball." I've played ball with a dog, but never with a parrot.

The parrot said, "I am serious, there is a lime-green tennis ball lying in the corner of the room. Please pick it up and bring it over here."

It was the type of tennis ball I used to use when I played high school tennis. I had a wicked serve then. I picked it up as requested. "Pop" as I used to call him, had already left the room. I wheeled myself out with the parrot perched upon my shoulder and entered a large cafeteria-style room which was filled with tables and people sitting around them. As much as I could see, they were all couples. The parrot had the tennis ball in its beak; this alone gives you an idea of the enormity of the bird. We were looking for the *right someone* to toss the ball to. We roamed around from room to room, there were several, but couldn't find that *someone* who was single. There were all couples present. Then the clock called me at my appointed hour of 5.00 a.m., and I awoke.

Some dreams are just that, dreams. They are garbled mish moshs' and bits and pieces of our subconscious or consciousness. Some dreams can be premonitions, and others are a means of the subconscious, superconscious, Self, Soul, Spirit or God speaking to us. This dream was a communication from some of the above.

Although sometimes my father often appears to be a personification of the Creator within, or the Divine Spark as it is often referred to in mystical literature, in this dream he appeared as a personification of my own spirit or Higher Self. He led me to a place deep within me where an aspect of my soul, the parrot was kept. This part of me, the emotional relationship with a female counterpart had not been pursued or activated for quite a while, or simply put; I had not been in a relationship for a very long, long time. "Would one expect less from a Lonely Mystic?" My soul and spirit have been busy exploring other aspects of my aim and purpose with great sacrifice, amusingly I might add. In the dream, the bird nipped my father once, but not the second time. This refers to my first long-term relationship which ended poorly. I was bitten pretty hard as a result of it.

Interestingly, I had a parrot at that time. Her name was Chiquita. She was a very gentle bird. Anyone could hold or touch her. She spoke several languages. After having owned her for a few years, one afternoon she took hold of my right index finger and refused to let go. I was shocked and panicked. I tried dislodging my finger from the grip of her jaw, but much to my dismay, she refused to let go. I shook my hand rapidly and she swung off striking the wall. I gently picked her up and placed her back into her cage. She just laid on bottom rungs without moving.

I was mortified. I had visions of having killed my parrot, my friend, and companion, but I had had no other choice. I needed my finger more than she needed to bite it off. While I was musing over my guilt, she revived and climbed up to her perch. I was in absolute agony over having hurt my friend and couldn't understand *Why did she attack me?* She was always such a gentle soul. I did a quick phone search and grabbed the cage with her in it. I placed the cage in the back seat of my coupe, secured it and then raced to a nearby animal hospital.

Needless to say, there were not too many people in the waiting room walking in with a caged parrot. After a long wait, the front desk asked me to bring the parrot up to the counter. After a thorough interrogatory, they took my parrot from me. In hindsight, I was quite surprised they didn't ask me for her Medicare card. After all, she was quite old. Oh, I forgot they wanted payment in advance. As soon as I handed over the cash, the bird looked at me squawked out her name and said the only Hebrew word she knew, "Shalom." Then she swung around, hung upside down from her perch for a moment and then dropped to the bottom of the cage.

My heart sank, and my face was on fire. I looked at the receiving administrator and said, "At least tell me why she died?" After about a half hour, the Vet came out and told me that she did not die due to a blow caused by me after having dislodged her from my finger. That blow hit the lower portion of her beak. He said, "Upon examining her, I've determined she died from a brain tumor."

I was devastated but vindicated. My heart took a deep breath. I said, "Goodbye old friend." I asked them if they could keep the cage. It was filthy anyway, *who wanted to clean the cage of a dead bird?* I had a tough enough time cleaning up my own apartment. I had no intentions of purchasing a new parrot anytime soon. Of course, I still carried around the guilt of having hurt her, even if she was ill. I found a way to resolve that guilt a week later.

Free Fall

It was a beautiful, cloudless summer day. I had no care in the world. I was riding my expensive foreign bicycle and for no apparent reason, while making a left turn, I went flying off the bike and landed on my chin, skidding while dragging my chin along with me.

At that time bicycle helmets were unrequired, as well as being unheard of. I did quite a number on my chin, but this I didn't know until I walked the bike back to my parent's house and rang the doorbell. Pop opened the door and turned white. My mother came over and almost toppled over. Pop had to catch her from reeling.

I shouldn't have walked into the bathroom to look at myself in the mirror, but I did. Half of my chin was hanging down. I tore off my tee shirt and propped it under my chin pressing the ripped portion back to the upper portion. Pop brought me one of his button-down collared shirts to put on and rushed me to the hospital. The emergency room admitted me pretty quickly, but they proceeded to do a terrible job of stitching my chin back together again. Twenty-six jagged stitches still adorn my chin. Sometimes it gets mistaken for a cleft chin. I was laid up on my back for a week until it started healing. I no longer felt guilty for having hurt my parrot.

The Scar

The scar is still visible, although I often cover it with a goatee, sometimes I wear it proudly. My first major relationship caused a deeper scar within me. One that pushed this aspect of my being into hiding, and kept it there under wraps, tucked far away within the confines of a highly complex structure, which was built up over many years. The first scar occurred years after the parrot had bitten me. I subsequently had plenty of time for it to collect dust and be kept under wraps. As to details of that "first bite" well…

Honey

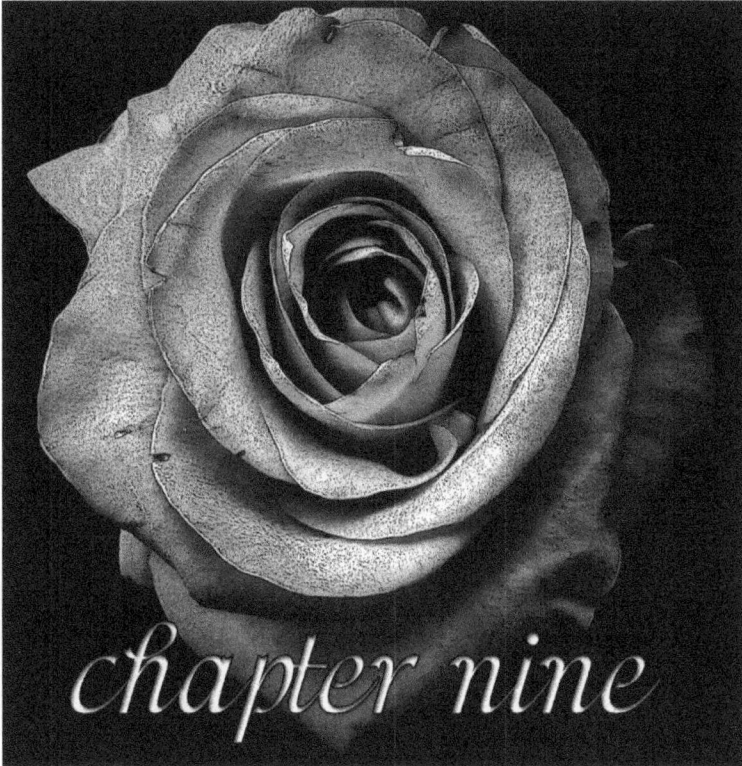

chapter nine

Who says a dream
Is just a dream?
Perhaps it is,
Just another chance.

The first time I saw him, I was almost asleep. The second time, that I saw him, I was asleep — almost.

A psychic had told me about him a while ago. She had said he was trying to get my attention about something. About what, she didn't know, but she said, "It would become very clear to you once you did see him."

To put it mildly, summer living in the country is filled with a cornucopia of insects. There are bugs that I can't even begin to describe. There are alien looking species and most probably are exactly that. "How do we know any different?" Just because they may be here before us doesn't mean they came from here. They come in all sizes and shapes. They fly, they crawl, they climb, they bore, they hide, and they race to name, but a small few of their qualities. They are highly inventive, highly dexterous and can act in unison or individually. Of course, this brief descriptive is totally intended for city folk that really do not interact with the hordes.

The Time of the Ants

The first time I saw them in unison I almost jumped out of my skin. Mom was over at my house that weekend, I know, "what a good son," you say. I went to select a DVD for the evening when I saw a black moving line in my office trailing from the closet door to the window wall. I quickly turned on the lights. As soon as the light hit the floor, I almost screamed. Fearing that Mom would get a coronary, I resisted the urge. Major control here, I might add. There were hundreds of black ants marching in a single line from the closet to the wall and vice versa. Mind you, this is a born and bred city boy from the big city, Manhattan, no less. I've had my share of cockroaches, bed bugs and boll weevils infestations. Yes, boll weevils in Manhattan. And yes, that may be another tale. But I've seen these army ants outside the house, but now they invaded my personal space in droves. I could have sworn I saw one wearing an army fatigue leaf helmet as well as holding an acorn-shaped bullhorn in his left clipper! It might have been my glasses; they are pretty scratched up, or maybe not. Soldier ants, all marching with tree splinter rifles between their two claw mustaches.

I kept it under wraps, so Mom wouldn't know, or she would come running in and we would have to make an unplanned trip to the nearby hospital. Something I didn't want to do again. A deer on the road had caused that to happen the first time Mom came to visit. I did not need an encore performance.

I told mom I had to go throw out the garbage and that I would be back from there shortly. This she was used to since I went to the local transfer station to unload every Saturday morning. I made sure not to set the house alarm to on as I had absent-mindedly done previously and almost had to escort the police away. I quickly raced over to the local hardware store, within the speed limit, of course. I didn't need that costly white slip. I purchased some powder to douse the carpet and ants with.

When I returned to the house, all was well and as I entered my office, I looked down. As you would have it, they were gone: "Zilch, nada, nothing!" It was as if they knew their demise was imminent. I proceeded to place several lines of the powder stretching across the carpet in the area that I last had seen them. Then I did something I shouldn't have done: Yep, you guessed it! I opened the closet door.

Now they were not in a line but in a puddle. A huge, swarming black gyrating, and spinning circle. I quickly started dumping the powder on them and them.

I could hear Mom yelling in the distance, "Did you fall asleep in there?"

I yelled, "No, I'll be right there."

She yelled, "Is everything OK?"

I didn't answer.

Mom is major high maintenance. God bless her! She is both challenging and challenged. Challenging because she inevitably could get under your skin, and make it boil. Not, that in any way she was malicious, malevolent, or ornery. This just was her nature. Lions "Rooooooar," they do not go "Meow." Wolves howl, they don't go "Woof, woof." And giraffes are speechless, not because they have nothing to say, but they have nothing to say it with. Some of us are what we are, fully. Mom was such. She also liked challenging herself constantly. She loved to grow, to learn, to experience and to teach. She taught me all the time, especially when I already knew what she was teaching, or if I had no desire to learn or listen to what she had to say. And of course, there were the times that she taught me much: Like how to take photographs and how to play guitar, how to dance, how to cook and how to love. Later in life, she also shared some of her deep spirituality with me. Something, which was hidden from most of her family life. But one day, she allowed it to come out. If it wasn't this, it would be that. It was one of those major stomach/bowel issues that prompted her experience with the Divine, a future tale.

We both enjoyed the movie. Of course, we watched it in my office. Yes, the stomping ground of the hordes. They were in the closet within a few feet of us. The office had the 3D TV and that was a real treat for her. It must have been divine intervention. Not one ant crossed the floor. I was watching that area more than the movie. I had already seen the movie and wanted to make sure I didn't have my own real-life adventure film being enacted on site. One hour into the film, Mom dozed off. We retired early for the night early, happily, I might add.

The next day when I opened the door, there were *no* ants present. In fact, they were not anywhere to be seen, but I had my suspicions. I believe I have unpaid tenants squatting within my walls. "No," you say? Really, I jest not! I believe I have a multi-unit, low income, rent-free condo in the rafters. But you know what they say, "Out of sight, out of mind." I have bigger fish to fry, or in this case "flying fish of sorts."

Weeks later, I noticed a sand pile developing in front of one of my trees. I went down to look and again I couldn't believe what I saw. There they were again, in droves! Now they had become contractors. The ringleader was still wearing the helmet, but this time it was a bright yellow acorn. He was directing hoards of them to excavate a hole in one of my larger trees. The sawdust was pouring out of it, and they were pouring into it. I felt violated again. Not as severely as when they were in the house, but still. I didn't know what to do, so I left it alone and figured nature would take its course. I now know I could have poured diatomaceous earth onto them, but who knew where they would have wound up next? Perhaps at your place? I'm sure you wouldn't want that, "Right?"

Two weeks later I found out where they did wind up next because they attacked again. This time I found them in droves beneath one of my metal garbage cans. I grabbed for the powder and spray and dosed them again. I could swear the ringleader was wearing a yellow poncho, a hood over his head and goggles over his eyes. How did he know I was going to douse and spray him? Those little buggers are so clever.

I didn't need them eating up my wood deck as they had done to the tree. Occasionally I still find one or two scouts surveying around. They are dressed in green fatigue, which easily blends into my beige and green kitchen tiles.

Having a discerning eye, one of the many gifts I inherited from Pop, I am easily able to spy them crawling. Pop was able to catch something wrong from miles away and make sure to point it out, in detail. I yelled and stomped, on them. I figured *if they didn't return to that well dressed, many hats and coated general of theirs, he would assume the enemy was too difficult to defeat and he would retreat and withdraw.* I felt like the guy that pounds his chest and let's loose a distinctive loud cry. I know who you are thinking about; I, however, was referring to one of my former schoolteachers.

That was the *Time of the Ants.* I have had several "Times" in and around the house. There were four other major ones; the *Time of the Flies and Moths, the Time of the Bees, the Time of the Grasshoppers and the Time of the Woodpeckers.* This tale is about the grasshoppers and bees followed by the Time of the Woodpeckers. As to the *Time of the Flies and Moths*, perhaps another time.

The Time of the Grasshoppers

In many ways, I'm a wimp. What we truly believe subconsciously is not necessarily what we manifest externally. "Wish one may, wish one might" when push comes to shove the *who* we think we are may run out of sight.

The first time lightning struck a tree across the pond and the tree fell, I felt as if a part of me had been injured. I mourned the death of the tree. I missed the place in the landscape it had occupied. I missed the image it had contributed to the overall beauty of the view. I was innocent and one with the land, with the air, and the house I lived in. All of this was sacred to me. Having lived for thirty-five years in the same apartment and now living in the country was as if I had arrived at a personal Nirvana. The death of a tree was an event to be mourned, and it was a trauma to be dealt with. I overcame.

When I first noticed the holes in the roof of my "A" frame house, it didn't dawn on me as to whom or what was redecorating my property. Then I remembered my father telling me about how bees had bored into his wooden house and how they had to call maintenance to come and visit in order to put poison in the excavated holes followed by covering them up. I turned around when I remembered this and yelled, "Maintenance" several times. Surprisingly, *No one came? Perhaps it was because I was in the woods?*

I could see the flying drill sergeants teaming around the roof. I could hear them sometimes and noticed them crawling in and out of my now multi-national low-income housing structure. I wondered if I could get a tax deduction for having undocumented aliens living in my house, "They were another life form weren't they?" Then it occurred to me that if I reported them, the alien police would show up and who knew what other undocumented creatures they might find living here? I figured *better to keep it to myself.*

I now had a mission, actually, one of several: To find a handyman that would come and fill the holes that the bees were making. But that wasn't the major reason I needed him. I was to discover that reason when I walked down to my partially finished ground floor the next day.

I have a home theater room: One of my pride and joys. Like the fallen tree, my innocence was invaded once more: This time by alien looking jumping things. As soon as I walked down the stairs, I could see a bunch of them jumping around on the carpet. *No problem,* I thought. I grabbed the bug spray and went after them. *Got 'em,* all five of them. Like chasing chickens around the yard, one by one they fell. I felt vindicated again, but something told me that I should take a closer look and visit the back-unfinished portion of the floor. Concurrently, something also told me not to take a look in that back portion. If I didn't go back there then there would be no story and subsequently, I most probably would have had to call the National Guard in to remedy the situation.

I gingerly walked in being very careful as to where I stood so I wouldn't step on one of them. Being very surprised, I did not notice even one of them on the floor. I sighed with relief. *What a dope!* I walked farther in and had surveyed the entire room: "Nothing!" I was free of those strange looking leggy buggers. *How stupid!* It was then the voice that voices things within me very, very quietly whispered, "Slowly look up, but do not freak-out!" Yes, it is a gentle, caring voice.

Needless to say, there was going to be something up there, which was going to freak me out big-time. Otherwise, why would that voice say, "Don't freak-out?" I know sometimes my logic is astounding. It was like hearing a spoiler to a movie or TV show.

Of course, you now know who the villain is. The spoiler just told you. *What fun is there in watching now?* But this wasn't a TV show, it was real life and I was about to come face to face with one of my arch nemeses: *I hate bugs!*

If I had been wearing a hat, it would have been better. I could have borrowed a helmet from the ant general, but he was buried deep within that excavated tree. Put politically correct, I am follically challenged, put in English (I know a dying language.) I have a bald head. Skin exposed, vulnerable, out there, and without a hat, unprotected. Outside I wear the hat, inside who would have figured? I slowly looked up, while holding my breath.

My blood pressure most of shot up by at least fifty points. I could feel the heat rise up to my face and accumulate in my cheeks, turning them a bright red. I could feel my pulse start racing and sweat start profusely pouring from every pore. My skin began to itch, my eyes started watering and my mouth went dry. My tongue desperately searched to moisten my lips with now vacant saliva, but I feared to open my mouth.

There were literally hundreds of those jumping hoppers hanging from the unfinished ceiling decked out on the insulation material hanging above. I could swear that all of their beady little eyes pivoted towards me, in unison. I could have been mistaken; the moment was traumatic. Their pesky little mustaches started twitching. Half on one side started sharpening their pointed feet, then the other half, their pointed hands. They were getting ready to pounce and attack me in unison. I could feel it. I could sense their microscopic brains churning and receiving directives from the leader of the pack to prepare to jump on their enemy, yours truly. Their general wasn't wearing a helmet; she was wearing a large, brimmed, woven, Panama hat with a yellow flower adorning it. I knew they could smell my perspiration and taste the anxiety pumping out from my wimpy demeanor.

What to do, what to do? Funny isn't it how that quiet voice was now silent. *Where was it when I needed it most?* A few seconds ago it was a big shot; sending SOS signals to an unprepared city slicker ill-equipped for country skirmishes. I figured it had the wits scared out of it too, even though it had told *me* not to freak-out. *Or perhaps it took a potty break? Do they too have to pee up there?*

I ran into the front room which had the finished ceiling, the one in the back had the unfinished ceiling. I grabbed the flying insect spray, pulled my tee shirt over my nose and mouth, then went ballistic on the ceiling. I sprayed and sprayed, strategically maneuvering myself so the falling hoard didn't land on my naked head: So much for strategic maneuvering. It was raining aliens in my basement. They were falling on my head, my bare arms, and my shirt. If I would have had to create a multicolor, multimedia nightmare, I couldn't have done a better job than life was now manufacturing for me.

I ran out of the room and plummeted into the fresh air. I breathed and breathed. I stood there staring blankly into the distance for quite a while and was glad no one had telephoned me. Not that anyone calls me anyway. I went up the stairs.

It wasn't until the next day that I ventured down again. This time I was armed with a construction hat, yellow poncho raincoat and rain boots that the General had loaned me. It would have been quite a picture for someone to take: Me wearing my grasshopper investigative garb. I looked like a governmental worker dressed in one of their white decontamination suits, except mine was yellow and green.

I looked around at the ceiling: Nothing? They were all on the floor. Dead, dead, dead. Did I say, "They were all dead?"

I swept them up and dumped them. I then proceeded to look around to see where and how they might have entered into the house: Maybe they came in the same way as the ants or mice? Oops, did I say, "Mice?" Slip of the tongue. (Mom might be reading this.) It was then I noticed that on the wall, where the oil tank connected to the outside pipe, the wall around the pipe was cut out and sealed with cement. Even though I'm not an architect or building inspector, it still dawned on me that the outside cinder blocks should be sealed around the outside of the house pipe too. "Smart thinking," you say. Yes, I know. I read minds.

I went outside and crawled under the deck to look at where the pipe that fills the oil tank enters the house. *Bingo!* All around the pipe, it was completely unsealed and open. *How could a contractor leave this so?* I had found the origin of Incognito Highway. This was the opening tunnel to the inside of my woes.

I was able to find a handyman that agreed to crawl under the deck to seal the pipe around. I paid him in advance. While I was at work, in addition to sealing the pipe opening he was to going to seal up the bee holes during the week. A lesson learned. No matter how honest or trustworthy the person appears "Do not pay in advance for work to be done in the future." If you pay, it means the work was done, even if it wasn't done. The *tunnel to trauma* was sealed, but the *holes to honey* weren't.

The Time of the Bees

In the fall I have a repetitive battle with my gutters. The leaves fill them and I clean them. The leaves fill them and I clean them. The leaves fill them and I clean them. In the summer, however, I have little reason to pay attention to them or the gutter pipes that lead from them. *Why would I?* They need attention in the fall, not the summer. There are no falling autumn leaves in the summer, but then again, *nature abhors a vacuum.*

Occasionally I would look up to the outside of the house. This time when I did so, I noticed some hornets flying around; they like building their nests up high in the alcove of the A-frame roof. This time, however, it was not the area of concern. It would have taken a lot to get me to check around in the area I was supposed to look to see what I was supposed to find. It would have to take something out of the ordinary. It would have to take something that would really need to catch my attention. Surprise to me, that *something* got my attention. The psychic was right.

My great room has a very high ceiling. Right in the middle of the room is a couch. Sleeping on that couch, in that room, in the middle of the woods is a healing experience. The first time my family came over for Thanksgiving, they all fell asleep on the couches before they even had any turkey. That's how high the vibes were in there. Needless to say, sleeping there was a treat: A special event. An event I tried to pursue when I could, which was usually on Saturday afternoons. Saturday afternoons are a perfect time for naps. That Saturday was no different.

The First Visitation

I made myself comfortable on the couch and covered myself with the blanket. It wasn't cold in the room, but if I awoke without the blanket over me I would be cold when I did awake. Many times I could feel my astral body leaving or entering during those interim moments. I laid it out expertly and folded it exactly as needed: Doubled of course, so that it fit the width of the couch as well as its length. I positioned my head, my hands, and my legs the way I was accustomed to. I carefully slid under it. I preferred left over right, but that caused cramps so I opted for the next best option: Right over left. I closed my eyes, said my prayers and started to drift into *La-La Land*.

A whole two and a half seconds must have passed when I found myself staring through the glass doors of the house; looking outside at the deck. There are ten doors. I was looking through the right ones facing the front side of the house. There, big as life, I saw a honey-colored, longhaired bear propped up on its hind legs.

It was smiling and looking at me as it turned around the corner of the deck. I said to myself in a panic, *there's a bear on my deck! What to do?* The fact that he was smiling didn't seem to register with me at all.

I started raising myself up when I realized my eyes were still closed? I had seen the event, as I was between waking and dream state. There had been a bear on the deck just as the psychic had predicted. Well, not a physical bear, but a bear, nonetheless. The energy was very high in the room and my body was aching for sleep, I could hardly keep my eyes open, I had to drift out, or should I say *in*.

When I awoke an hour later, it was still daylight and I was determined to go out on to the deck and check if there was something out there which I needed to pay attention to. After all, that was what my new messenger was trying to tell me, "Right?" *Why else would a smiling bear be walking around on my deck?*

It was difficult to get up from and off of that couch. Difficult, not because the couch was at fault, difficult, because of the lushness of the pillows and their close proximity to the coffee table; which happened to be positioned right next to it. After several attempts, I did so accompanied by some snapping and cracking of vertebra and joints that bore witness to the event. I finally arose, visited the facilities and then with great trepidation, I might add, I went out onto the deck.

I turned the first corner, not the one I had seen him turn, and then arrived at the second corner. I suppose a part of me may have half expected to see a bear out there, although the greater part of me didn't expect that at all. One morning, while I was driving to work, I had seen a live black bear on a mountain, but that was quite a distance from here. When I arrived around the bend, there was no bear. There was nothing. Nothing that is, until I did a thorough examination of everything on that part of the deck. It was then I saw it. I stepped back catching my breath.

There below the gutter and sandwiched between the drainpipe and the wall of the house was a humongous webbed cocoon of some kind. I had seen a hornets' nest, a wasp's nests, but this was way, way bigger and weirder looking than all of those put together. It was kind of like an alien cocoon that was hot pepper shaped and wrapped in web-like wrappings. It was suspended and securely tied into the gutter pipes, which ran along the side of the house directly on its corner and attached to the gutter. It was well entrenched in its hiding spot. It was brilliant insect subterfuge and camouflage. *Did they go to architecture school to learn how to do this?* We have to train to get the skills needed to do construction on a similar basis, *where do they get it from? What to do?* Crossed my mind again quite strongly.

I acted impulsively, intuitively, promptly, stupidly and spontaneously: All of the above in an instant. I grasped the handle of a nearby broom that was propped up against the cord of my firewood and began banging the pipe, quite violently. After several strategically aimed hits, the cocoon was dislodged. I so had hoped that whatever was in there was deep, deep in *Beddy-bye Land.*

Luckily for me it, they, or them were. With the best hockey puck strike I could muster up, I swept the thing off of the deck. *Wham!* It went flying through the poles of the deck as if a trophy master had landed one right through the goalie's legs, straight into the woods. *Finito suckers!*

My four-legged honey bear had saved me and averted a potential mishap in the future. How severe it may have been of course was unknown, but it most probably would have been significant or it wouldn't have registered on the "psychic net."

One would think that having associated such a memorable, positive experience within myself with this *new protector* would have somehow have opened the door for me to a new trust level with similar *animal protectors*, but unfortunately such was not the case.

Visitation Number Two

It seems that the time in between waking and dream state is a treasure trove of experiences for me or for that matter many if they choose to explore them. I vacillate between wanting to be aware of them and wanting to be oblivious to them. When things are going well, I pay attention. When they are not, I don't. I don't, that is until I would be looking for some answers from the inner realms to questions about what is or isn't occurring in waking state.

Years later I saw him again.

I was sleeping and was about to wake up. I saw him walk over towards me. The bear got down on all fours. First, he lowered his head; and then crouched down and touched the bottom of his chin to the floor. His paws were laid down, and his belly was resting on the ground. His eyes were wide open. I say "his," because I had the sense that it was a "he" and not a "she." I could have been mistaken.

He was in a posture of sublimation, a position that stated, *I am safe; I am not here to threaten you.* I know he wanted me to put my hand on his head the way you acknowledge a dog or a cat. He wanted me to show him that I trusted him enough to connect with him. He wanted me to let him into my life in ways that were closed to him before. My hand ached to touch that furry snout. I could deeply feel it in the core of my being. I could taste it and feel the longing to do so in my chest. His was a simple request. On my part, it could have been a so simple a response. The slightest of a gesture, just a simple, gentle touch, not even a lingering one. A quick one would have done just fine. It would have shown him and all those others that assist me that I had grown up and that I was ready. I withdrew my already slightly extended hand. *How sad.* I was still afraid. I woke up.

Sometimes you can hide who you are from others, but you can't hide who you are from yourself. Your inner self knows you very, very well, even better than you think you know you. It structures events so that you learn to know yourself too. These subconscious fears that block you are not matters of consciously deciding to overcome them and go "poof" so that they are obliterated. Yes, positive thinking and programming, work, but real change has to come from very deep within or high above: From even deeper than deep. And you need help to get there. Hopefully, one day I will be able to pet my honey bear. Until then I will have to settle for a small token of my affection and willingness to try to get closer to him, again.

I placed that token on the altar in my great room, in a small silver cup and keep it there in case he comes back and wants to give me another chance: It's filled with, *honey*.

Who

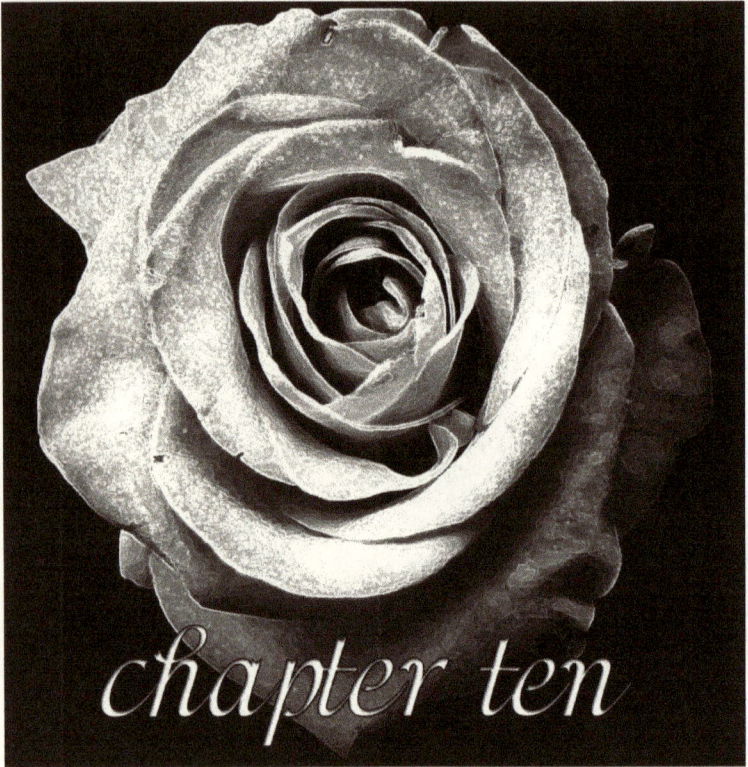

chapter ten

Was that *who* or *whom*
You said was calling?

I've heard that cackle before.

It was a Saturday morning TV sound I grew up with and I knew well. It was a mocking sound. It was a call that challenged the validity of your territorial rights. A persistent red-headed maleficent creature plagued my country home during my first year of ownership.

As an adult, I had no need for an alarm clock on a Saturday morning: Nope, none at all. Yet, like clockwork, at 5:00 a.m. there was a loud pounding that resonated from somewhere in the house, or so I thought. The first time it happened I plummeted out of bed as if I had heard an air raid siren go off. I practically jumped down the entire flight of stairs, which lead down to the great room. I frantically searched all over, *where was that tumultuously loud banging sound coming from?* It was resonating throughout the entire house: An incessant, repetitive tapping. I raced down another flight of stairs to the boiler thinking *perhaps it was broken and was crying out for attention?* Nope, not there either. I was at a loss and out of my element.

Country living was new to me. Owning a house was new to me. Having a house turn into an alarm clock was new to me. I was overwhelmed, underprepared and inundated with anxiety, mystery, and lack of sleep. City mornings were early wakes, having to be at work by 7:30 a.m., but a 5:00 a.m. wakeup call, when I was sleeping at my country oasis for the weekend was much more than

I planned for or had ever expected to experience.

More than anything, I looked forward to a long, leisurely, deep and restful sleep on Saturday mornings. Bringing the garbage to the local transfer station could always wait until 11:30 a.m. There were no other chores that required my immediate attention. Other than a check in see-if-all-was-OK call with Mom, but that too could wait. So a 5:00 a.m. bugle call was a head shuddering, huff, and puff, downright physical attack on my serenity.

Luckily, it always only lasted for only about five minutes. Then it stopped. It started early spring and lasted two months: Two months of having a house dictate my sleep patterns. I almost considered sleeping at my apartment in the city on weekends instead of visiting my home away from home. Then, after weeks of deep deliberation, I questioned everyone that I knew who happened to own a house, for suggestions on how to deal with this. Deeply frustrated I decided to venture outside at 5:00 a.m.

Somehow, the thought had occurred to me that the origin of the sound was not coming from inside of the house, but from its outside. I suspect that one of my friends, "upstairs" was whispering that into my brain. When I say "upstairs," I don't mean people living above me. Well, they are maybe above me, but they aren't living. I was referring to the spiritual beings that assist us. I walked onto the deck and began circling the house. It was then I happened to look up at the chimney of the house.

The Pileated One!

Eureka! I thought. Mystery solved, but not the problem. The problem was now defined and the quest to solve or cure it had begun: All of this because of a single glance at the metal flue protruding from my wooden chimney. All those months of wonder, suffering, discomfort, and agitation evaporated because now I had a new aim and purpose. Now I had a mission. Now I had a quest. Now I had become a covert operative that was on an assignment.

"What was this?" you ask.

I respond: "To find a way to get that tall, beautiful, large black pileated woodpecker with a red-orange crew cut off of, and permanently away from, my house!"

And to make matters worse, upon seeing me, it, him, her, them, and whatever let loose that magical cackle, it let loose that iconic laughter which mocked me saying: "You idiot. Do you really think you can stop me from banging on your flue and waking you up anytime that I want, any day that I want, or any way that I want? You city slicker dummy!" I could swear I heard those words. Well...

It stopped banging, turned its head slowly and deliberately and looked me straight in the eyes. If its beak could smile then it would be smiling. It let that cackle loose again as it flew off into the woods, eying me all the time.

I was breathless. I was dumbfounded, I was, *well what can I say?* The deed to the house did not include him. They were *my* acres of land. Where did he get the nerve to encroach upon my territory, my house, my sacred property and lay claim to "his" territory? By clanging on the flue, he was declaring to the world, "Hey everybody, this place is mine and you had better stay the heck away or I will peck you and send you packing."

I actually went back to sleep that morning and for the first time since the ordeal had begun; I woke up at 10:30 a.m. I was refreshed and on a mission to find a way to rid myself of him.

Pileated woodpeckers are endangered species and cannot be harmed. My nemesis was protected. I could do him no hurt, harm or injury. So, given that, *how could I convince him to go elsewhere after he had so loudly claimed my domicile as his house*? I do not speak Spanish yet, nor did I ever invite him in by offering *Me Casa, Su Casa*. I did what any respectable new homeowner would do; I asked my best friend when it came to issues like this: The Internet. The Internet and I have a long history. I had a thirty-page multi-media site up advertising my albums of music when one of the largest software giants only had one page up with promises to have more. Like other things, I didn't pursue it.

I searched and searched. I contacted several pest control specialists that offered me a host of $1,000.00 solutions. All of them were "deterrents" and were not guaranteed to work. They were going to spray tacky stuff up there; they were going to do this and do that and then charge me an arm and a leg. I decided to keep my arms and legs intact. I prayed heavily for a solution. I tend to do this when I am faced with situations that are way beyond my control, expertise, and know-how. My prayers were answered.

On a fine, and memorable day, although I forget the specifics, the mind isn't what it used to be. I suspect due to all those early Saturday mornings. On that fine day, at 5:00 a.m. and out of sheer frustration and anger, I picked up a rubber mallet. It had been lying with the fireplace tools and began pounding on the inside of the flue the same number of times that I heard the bird pecking on the outside of it. As if a magical incantation had been recited by a host of visiting angels, as if a group of mages had chanted verses of protection and evacuation, as if a celestial net had descended upon the culprit and forcibly removed it sending it to another dimension, place and time, my unwelcome visitor ceased its banging.

I ran outside and saw it vacate the chimney, cackling as it exited left, or maybe right, who remembers at this point. I was delirious with delight, euphoric with happiness and fully satiated with feelings of triumph, accomplishment, and contentment.

It is funny how difficulties create a place and space in our lives, which although being negative and uncomfortable, none-the-less are still purposeful with meaning. The woodpecker's leaving not only removed all those previously scheduled Saturday mornings of discomfort but also created for me new opportunities, whatever they were going to happen to be.

I've heard it said, "Two things couldn't occupy the same place at the same time so." I must have overheard Pop telling Mom this when she tried to RSVP to two weddings. Both were being held at 6:00 p.m. on the same date, but at different halls. He said it in Yiddish, "*Mir kunish tanzen of tzviah chasenis mite ein tuchos.*" In case sensitive ears are listening a loose translation is, "One bottom can't dance on two weddings at the same time." The nemesis has occupied a place in my life for a long time. Now it was time for something new, but I did see him one last time after he *flew the flue.*

It was also on a Saturday, but this time late morning and while I was in a hurry to go shopping, I know, how pathetic. I exited the house and did a quick walk-around on the deck. It was there that I saw him lying on the floor of the deck next to the swinging bench. What had happened to him was a mystery. *How did he wind up on the deck there for me to see? Very strange* I thought. I told myself that when I returned I would give him a proper burial after all bygones are bygones. He was a magnificent bird and deserved a proper burial. In the event that he was still alive and needed to drink, I went inside and filled a small glass dish with water. I slowly pushed the dish next to his beak and left. He didn't budge.

I returned later that afternoon. I went over to the barn and found a shovel and then walked up to the deck and around to where I had seen him earlier. He was gone. The small glass bowl was overturned. I don't know if he flew off somewhere. Occasionally birds fly into the large windows of my house. Perhaps he had done so and suffered only a momentary stun, which caused him to plummet below. Perhaps he was then transported by something to somewhere else, for some other purpose. Don't know. But I did know I was done with him, or at least I thought I was.

There are other types of woodpeckers besides pileated ones. I was done with these pesky buggers for quite a few years. I thought I had ended that chapter in my life and this book. Of course, it would be on a Saturday morning that I happened to walk around the deck. I usually had done so before I went to the transfer station. It was then I noticed wood chips scattered all over the floor of the deck, directly below the pointed alcove framing my roof. I reluctantly looked up and saw white markings on the part of the roof, which protruded, beyond the side of the house. I also saw scratch marks on the side of the house, which was directly under the roof.

Night Birds

I was romantically dining outside at a tourist spot in Nevada. It was near dusk time. My companion and I looked around. There was no one seated outside in the plush, beautifully decorated outdoor garden dining spot. When we had arrived, the owner had offered to seat us in the restaurant, but my companion (Yes. I know. Hard to believe for The Lonely Mystic, but I have on rare occasions had one.) said, "No, I like the way the outside garden looks." The owner questioned her and said, "Are you sure?" This seemed strange to me at the time, but what did I know? I was a city slicker, and we were out in the wide-open spaces.

The waitress gave us the menu and asked us if we would like to go inside. But again, my companion insisted saying, "No." We ordered from what looked like an exquisite menu and sat there chitchatting and discussing the events of the day. It was then that I first saw something dart across the already almost dark sky. It was dusk. The garden spot was already dimly lit up. At first, I saw one, and then two and then three. I immediately knew what they were, even though it was my first experience with "Night Birds." The waitress came over with her eyes up to the sky, rather than us. She said to my companion again, "Are you sure you don't want to go and dine inside?" Again my companion insisted, "No."

I turned to her and said, "Did you see anything flying across the sky a few moments ago?" I didn't want to cause her to panic.

She said, "Of course I did."

I said, "Well, do you want to go inside because of them?"

She said, "Why would I? Just because there are some night birds flying around is no reason to dine inside. It is a beautiful night."

The waitress was the one that broke the bad news to her. She said, "Honey, there are no such things as *night birds*. Dear, those are BATS!"

She said the magic word. My companion tore out from the table, as a bat from you know where. She grabbed her bag and yelled at me, "What kind of place did you take me to! Why did you want to sit outside?" Needless to say, we went inside after that.

Back at the country home, I saw bats flying around at dusk. They were my unsolicited and payment free form of pest control. They held my mosquito population in check. Having a pond in front of the house, I needed them to do their job and might add, they did it excellently. I ignored the fact that they used the recess below the roof to rest at night. In the morning I often found their droppings on the deck. But the scratch marks and wood shaving I saw on the deck were something new. I was now worried they had taken up permanent residence inside of the house.

I walked around to the front of the house and saw the same there. Something was trying to get in. Something was trying to invade my space again. I was under attack and now had a new mission. I assumed the stance of a man hunting for a solution. This was the posture of a covert operative doing background checks on ways to remedy the problem. Once again I consulted friends, relatives, and strangers in an attempt to find a way of dealing with this new attack. I called five different services to come and survey the issue and offer solutions. For some reason, their solutions all revolved around me dishing out $1,000.00 again and not getting any guarantee. $1,000.00 must be some kind of magic number that they are all taught before graduating from their respective universities.

They told me that I might have squirrels, raccoons, and assorted other vermin attacking my premises. I was overwhelmed once more. I thought my problems had vacated the premises when the woodpecker "flue" the coop to that big animal sanctuary in the sky.

Then the thought occurred to me: *Why don't I buy one of those outdoor hunting surveillance cameras that capture activity when no one is around.* I figured *if I knew what I was dealing with I might be able to more effectively deal with it.* I immediately went out and bought one. I loved spending money.

What's nice about spending money when you don't have it is that you can always return what you spent it on when you don't need it anymore. This I learned well when I was working at a store where customers would come in and purchase complete outfits only to return them after the weekend.

I set up the camera and after several days and nights found nothing recorded. Then one morning, when I was going out to check the camera, I saw *it*.

It looked so sweet, so pretty, and I thought, *how impishly malicious.* Of course, to him, there was no evil intent. To him, it was self-preservation. To him, it was a hunt for sustenance. To him, he was doing his due diligence and searching for food. To him, he was providing for his family and there were most probably many members. I wouldn't have been surprised if he was searching for those ants that had mysteriously disappeared on that now infamous evening.

They are back!

He was a small woodpecker with what looked like a blue streak or blue wings. He could have been a Blue Jay. He craftily inched his way over the side of the roof and peeked down to see what I was doing. I spied him doing so, being quickly alerted by a change of scenery up above. He quickly retreated the moment he saw me look at him. *Bingo!* I know knew what I was dealing with. I had just saved thousands of dollars and hours of aggravation. Now the question became *how do I deal with it? Again!*

A few weeks earlier, my great niece and her brother came visiting with their parents. She was enamored of one of the current cartoon movie characters as many children of similar age were, so I purchased a huge metallic helium-filled balloon for her. I tied it to the railing of the deck. She was completely delighted when she saw it.

"Out of the mouth of babes," they say. It hit me. *Buy several multicolor metallic balloons and suspend them near the roof. Perhaps this would deter the unwelcome guests from damaging my roof?*

I raced over to the local balloon store and purchased a half dozen of them. I tied them to the front of the house and the rear of the house. I cleaned the deck, so I would be able to tell if there were any new chips on the floor.

The wind was uncooperative. No sooner had I suspended the balloons than the wind rearranged them, tangling them into my trees or below my deck. I did more research. I discovered tape that could be purchased, but even more interesting were "owl balloons," which were offered as deterrents for woodpeckers. I suppose woodpeckers are afraid of owls. I did what any self-respecting consumer would do, I immediately ordered both the balloons and tape from my friend, you know who.

Two days later they arrived. I attached the tape to the railings of the deck, letting them flap in the wind and had the owl balloons inflated at the local owl-inflating store. Yes, some specialists do nothing but inflate owl balloons. It must be an epidemic.

I then tied the balloon to my railing in a manner that I hoped would preclude nature from interfering with. Several times a day I could see the woodpeckers scouting the house from high above. They were doing a fly-by. They were checking up on me to see what I was doing. "Incredible isn't it? Who would believe it? Who would think they were as smart as they were?"

I didn't see wood chips on the deck, nor did I hear them pecking on the underside of the roof. It appeared I had solved the issue again. As I said, it appeared like I had solved the issue again. Did I say it appeared as if I had solved the issue again?

The next day I heard banging coming from the flu. While the woodpeckers were deterred from the sides of the house, they now chose to attack the chimney once more. These weren't the pileated woodpeckers from before. Of course, I remembered the prior year's solution to a chimney attack and promptly banged on the flue. This caused them to *fly the coup*, again. They were gone, again. I was once more, elated, euphoric and totally pleased with myself. Mind you that these feelings were far and few in occurrences. Don't, even for a moment think I was used to such because I wasn't.

That night I meditated, as lonely mystics are prone to do. I felt quite well protected by the holographic tapes fluttering in the wind and owls hovering above. My guides have a great sense of humor. I love them. I don't mind they or even God sometimes make fun of me when they or He speaks with me. As I was starting to dive deep within, clear as day and loud as a bell as if it was right there in the room with me, I heard:

"Who!"

No. I don't have a pet owl.

Index of Titles

Extra Goodies

PORTRAITS OF A LONELY MYSTIC ILLUSTRATED NOVEL BOOK SERIES

THE LONELY MYSTIC
DISGUISED AS A COSMIC CHEF. ONE OF THE RARE
PHOTOS OF HIM WITHOUT A HAT!

THE LONELY MYSTIC

As Care Taker

WITH HIS YARD UTENSILS

WOODPECKER
MAKES A SPECIAL CAMEO APPEARANCE

EXCERPTED FROM
PORTRAITS OF A LONELY MYSTIC
DOUBLE TALK

THE LONELY MYSTIC

As Tiny Tyke, the saga begins

**"I'M NOT IN A STROLLER,
THIS IS A HIGH ROLLER!"**

EXCERPTED FROM
PORTRAITS OF A LONELY MYSTIC IN 3D

After-words

Flowers for my beloved, wherever she may be…

Postscript

It appears woodpeckers are not only able to fly well in strong rains, but they also know how to read short stories. I had written *Who* at a coffee shop earlier in the morning. It was a stormy day. I had long removed the tape and balloons that adorned my property since the birds had not bothered the house in quite a while. I entered my house and went up to the bedroom to change the bedding. It was then I heard that all too familiar repetitive tapping sound in stereo coming from the front of the house. I quickly ran over to the window. I peered out and to the right, I saw a rather large woodpecker doing his best to tear into the underside of the house. I banged on the window. He flew off. I started closing the window when a smaller one flew over to the left underside of the house and started pecking. I opened the window and as loud as I could I yelled, "Who!"

He quickly flew off. So far he hasn't come back, but I did suspend another owl balloon from the banister.

About the Author

Misha Ha Baka has worn many hats during his professional career. He has penned several other works including the poetry book of Confessions of a Lonely Mystic small talk and the illustrated fictional novels series, Portraits of a Lonely Mystic. He has a BA in English Literature, an MA in Asian Studies and has studied healing and mystic thought in Asia, England, Israel, and the United States. He is an ordained spiritual healer and ordained member of the clergy. He is a fine artist, a graphic artist, a photographer, a musician, and a composer with dozens of albums of original music including *Passion*, *Miracle*, and *Ancient*.

www.ingramcontent.com/pod-product-compliance
Lightning Source LLC
LaVergne TN
LVHW011241080426
835509LV00005B/581